GRAMMAR

CRANE HILL
PUBLISHERS

The Geek's Guide to Grammar

ISBN-13: 978-1-57587-255-1
ISBN-10: 1-57587-255-2

Design by Miles G. Parsons

Printed in the United States

Library of Congress Cataloging-in-Publication Data

Beam, Linda J.
   Geek's guide to grammar / by Linda J. Beam.
      p. cm.
   ISBN-13: 978-1-57587-255-1
   1. English language--Grammar. 2. English language--Usage.
I. Title.
PE1112.B38 2006
428.2--dc22

2006031136

THE GEEK'S GUIDE

GRAMMAR

Linda J. Beam

CRANE HILL
PUBLISHERS

CONTENTS

THE GEEK'S GUIDE

THE UNIVERSAL SKILL

Is there any skill more vital to getting along well in everyday life than good communication? Whether it's on a personal or professional basis, and whether we communicate by written or spoken word, we interact with people every day with our language skills.

To do this as effectively as possible, it just makes sense to want to do it as well as possible. After all, there is nothing more distracting than words obviously misused and language that makes us look backward or uneducated.

And let's face it, communication skills say a lot about a person. They tell people whether (or not!) you care to present yourself well, and as correctly as possible. They reveal whether you are careful or careless about the way you present yourself to others. This is especially critical on special occasions, say, for example, in job interviews, when your command of grammar might be the thing that makes the difference between a good impression or a poor one.

And here's something else to consider: No matter whether we are in a professional or personal setting, or even a social setting, our speech is often the first thing from which people form a first impression of us. Since it is true that "We never get a second chance to make a good first impression," it is imperative that we present ourselves as effectively as we can on every occasion. Often, we meet people first on the telephone or by e-mail, and the other person has nothing on which to form an opinion of us except our language.

The Geek's Guide to Grammar can help you present yourself correctly and effectively. It offers grammar do's and don'ts for even the most basic communication, but as the name implies, it offers you extra tips to make you a grammar geek. Geek chic! And that's a good thing! Who doesn't want to be more knowledgeable and extra-smart, especially about a skill that is used in every aspect of your life?

THE GOODS ON GRAMMAR

We'll begin our guide to geekdom with a review of the building blocks of our language, the parts of speech. After all, we need to know the basics and what to expect of them to know how they should interact correctly. Let's talk about what each part of speech is, what it does, and how it works with the other parts to make up correct language use.

If you're tempted to skip that review, let me remind you again of how important it is to have a strong foundation in language basics. It won't matter that you're a geek with a high I.Q. if your language skills make you look otherwise. Incorrect usage can make you look less knowledgeable than you are. How often have you seen TV and political personalities that mis-spoke and looked foolish as a result? At the very least, they weren't able to say what they meant. Some people even become known for their chronic misuse of English. Entertainer Norm Cosby, for example, built his comedic career around the misuse of words. Funny as he was, we hope he knew better in real life. Real geeks don't want to be laughed at. They want to be known for expressing themselves clearly and succinctly.

Act as smart as you are by knowing and using correctly the basics on the pages that follow.

NOTEWORTHY NOUNS

The first part of speech we'll consider is the **noun** — we use it more than almost any other part of speech.

Most people know what nouns are and what they do: They name things. We usually don't have trouble identifying those, at least the more common types.

But many people don't know that there are actually several different varieties of nouns, some that can't even be seen or touched. We'll need to know all the different kinds when we talk about choosing correct verbs to go with them, so let's do a quick review of the different kinds of nouns we might run across.

GEEK GLOSSARY

A **noun** names a person, place, thing, quality, idea, or action.

Types of Nouns

Nouns all name things, but there are different categories of the names they provide.

<u>Common</u> <u>nouns</u> give the names of everyday, ordinary, general things like car, town, and teacher. Used in sentences, they look like this:

- I drove my <u>car</u> to the lake this weekend.
- My <u>town</u> is having a big homecoming celebration.
- Our <u>teacher</u> gave us no homework for the weekend.

When we are specific in naming things, we use **proper** **nouns**. It's important to know and recognize these because they should be capitalized. Here's how proper nouns would look in the same sentences we used above.

- I drove my **Honda** to the lake this weekend.
- **Birmingham** is having a big homecoming celebration.
- **Mrs.** **Hannah** gave us no homework for the weekend.

GEEK GLOSSARY

Common nouns give general names like car and teacher.
Proper nouns name particular things, like Chevrolet and Mr. Johnson.

These words in bold name not just general things, but very specific ones, so they are capitalized. In a later chapter, we'll talk more about some other things that should be capitalized as well.

Concrete **nouns** name things that we can touch, feel, smell, or take in with our senses in any way. These sentences use **concrete** nouns.

GEEK *Speak:*

"A special kind of beauty exists which is born in language, of language, and for language."
Gaston Bachelard

- The **dog** ran quickly to his owner.
- The chef quickly prepared the **food** as we watched.
- The **book** was shipped as soon as it was published.

Abstract **nouns** name concepts, beliefs, and qualities that we cannot touch, but that are, nevertheless, very real. Just because we can't see them doesn't mean they aren't here. And what's more, they often appear in sentences, so we need to know how to recognize and treat them properly.

GEEK*Speak:*

"Words are as beautiful as wild horses, and sometimes as difficult to corral."

Ted Berkman

- We celebrate our <u>liberty</u> on July 4 each year.
- His <u>belief</u> in the system saw him through the ordeal.
- He found the <u>courage</u> he needed in the difficult situation.

<u>Collective</u> <u>nouns</u> name things that may be made up of a lot of individual things, but the whole is referred to as one unit. This is an important type of noun to know in our discussion of verbs.

Concrete nouns name things that can be touched, felt, or smelled. **Abstract nouns** name things that we cannot touch, like faith and hope.

- The <u>choir</u> sang with enthusiasm during the program.
- What decision did the <u>jury</u> make?
- The <u>city</u> decided to proceed with plans for the library.

There are some special things about nouns that we'll talk about in the following chapters, including how to make them plural.

Collective nouns name things referred to as one unit, but are made up of individual things, like choir and team.

- Nouns name things like book, car, and teacher.

- Nouns come in several varieties:

  - Common nouns name general things, like books.

  - Proper nouns name particular things, like *War and Peace*.

  - Concrete nouns name things that can be touched, like table.

  - Abstract nouns name things that cannot be touched, such as fear.

  - Collective nouns name a group that is made up of individual items, for example, faculty.

PLURALS WITHOUT PROBLEMS

Nouns go from being singular to plural in a variety of ways, depending on several things. Here are some guidelines to help with this process.

Most nouns can be **singular** (just one), or **plural** (more than one). They can be changed from singular to plural in a variety of ways.

To form the plural of most words, simply add an s.

Singular	Plural
paper	papers
table	tables
book	books

For words ending in s, z, x, sh, ch, or ss, add es to make the word plural.

Singular	Plural
kiss	kisses
buzz	buzzes
dish	dishes

 *Check to see the last letter of the word before deciding how to make it plural.*

For words ending in o, check to see what letter comes before the o.

If a vowel comes before the o, you will usually simply add an s.

Singular	Plural
cameo	cameos
rodeo	rodeos
stereo	stereos

If a consonant comes before the o, you will generally add es.

Singular	Plural
potato	potatoes
hero	heroes
veto	vetoes

But there are exceptions to this. Some words ending in o do not get the extra e.

Singular	Plural
zoo	zoos
piano	pianos
auto	autos

And, some words ending in o can be made plural either way.

Singular	Plural
cargo	cargos/cargoes
buffalo	buffalos/buffaloes

To make a word plural that ends in y, check to see if the letter right before the y is a vowel or a consonant.

If the letter before the y is a vowel, just add an s.

Singular	Plural
boy	boys
Sunday	Sundays

If the letter before the y is a consonant, change the y to i and add es.

Singular	Plural
lady	ladies
candy	candies
penny	pennies

To make a word plural that ends in f or fe, change the f to v and add es.

Singular	Plural
knife	knives
leaf	leaves
wife	wives

Note that there are some exceptions to this: <u>chef</u>, <u>cliff</u>, and <u>belief</u> are just a few.

 *Some words have completely different spellings in their singular and plural forms, and some look exactly the same.*

17

GUERRILLA GEEK

Mail call! People often incorrectly form the plural of their names for mailboxes, greeting cards, etc. In every case, the proper form can be made by adding only s or es to the name.

For names that do not already end in an s sound, just add s to the name.

Singular	**Plural**
Smith	Smiths
O'Neal	O'Neals
Johnson	Johnsons

For names that already end in an s sound, add es.

Singular	**Plural**
Douglas	Douglases
James	Jameses
Metts	Mettses

If you think the result looks odd, you can always reword, and say, for example, "The James Family," without adding anything directly to the name. Whichever way you choose, do not change the internal spelling of the name. For instance, with names that end in y, do not ever drop the y and add an i.

Some words don't seem to have any rhyme or reason for how their plurals are formed.

Singular	Plural
child	children
foot	feet
person	people

The good news is that some words are exactly the same, whether you use them as singular or plural!

Singular	Plural
deer	deer
series	series
sheep	sheep

And some aren't used at all except in a plural form.

Singular	Plural
pants	pants
pliers	pliers
scissors	scissors

 *For compound words, make the noun part of the combination plural.*

Singular	Plural
attorney-general	attorneys-general
chief-of-staff	chiefs-of-staff
mother-in-law	mothers-in-law

GEEK
AT A GLANCE

- Nouns may be either singular (just one), or plural (more than one).

- Plurals are formed in a variety of ways. To know which way is correct for a word, check to see the last letter in it. Sometimes you simply add an <u>s</u>, but sometimes you must add <u>es</u>. Other times, other letters are needed.

- Some words are the same, no matter if they are singular or plural, such as deer.

- Some words are plural, no matter if you mean one or more. An example would be scissors.

- For a very few words, there is no rhyme or reason on how to form their plural. An example would be child and its plural, children.

- To make compound words plural, make the noun part of the word plural. For example, attorney-general would become attorneys-general.

TAKING CARE OF YOUR POSSESSIONS

Nouns can be possessive, that is, they can show ownership, besides being singular or plural.

Here are some sentences that contain words showing ownership.

- The **boy's** mother picked him up from school early.
- John gave the **car's** engine a quick check before he left.

Making Simple Nouns Possessive

As we can see in the above sentences, the way most nouns will be made possessive when they do not already end in an **s** is simply to add **'s**.

Noun	Possessive Noun
book	book's
house	house's

 *Most singular nouns can be made possessive by simply adding **'s**.*

This even works when the nouns are already plural and do not end in an **s**.

Noun	Possessive Noun
children	children's
feet	feet's
men	men's

Now we get to the part that real geeks want to know about:

"How do you make a word possessive when it already ends in s?"

There is not one simple answer to this. Experts and stylebooks differ. What we'll do here is to present several ways to handle this, and you can decide which you prefer.

Some grammarians

GUERRILLA GEEK

Some idiomatic expressions (commonly accepted terms that really don't follow the rules of grammar) always have an apostrophe even though they don't actually indicate possession of anything. Examples include <u>**a stone's throw**</u>, <u>**an hour's wait**</u>, and <u>**at wit's end**</u>. Every language has such terms.

suggest that this is not complicated at all. If the word already ends in an <u>s</u>, whether the word is plural or singular, just add an apostrophe.

- <u>**Kansas'**</u> legislature
- <u>**Dickens'**</u> novels

That's certainly the simplest choice, so you may want to do that.

Other experts say that when the noun ends in <u>s</u>, you should still simply add <u>'s</u>. It may look unusual to you, but it is acceptable. Here's what that would look like.

- <u>**Kansas's**</u> legislature
- <u>**Dickens's**</u> novels

Finally, other authorities suggest that if the word ending in **s** is **singular**, like **news**, you should still add **'s**. If the word ends in **s** because it is **plural**, then just add an apostrophe.

- *Birmingham News's* lead story (singular word ending in **s**)
- **Doctors'** office (plural word ending in **s**)

There are, of course, notable exceptions. For example, there is no need to add the extra **s** when it would result in two or more syllables that end in the eez sound. Here are some examples:

- **Euripides'** tragedies
- For **Jesus'** sake

When you use a possessive pronoun in the place of a noun, do not include an apostrophe. For example, do not use apostrophes with these substitutes that show ownership.

- The car is **his**.
- The pupil was one of **hers**.
- **Its** color was a bright red.

*No matter which way you choose to show possession of a word already ending in **s**, the most important thing is to be consistent. Choose a method and stick with it each time you form a possession.*

Even if there would be no awkward *sound* if you add **'s**, you may still use only the apostrophe if the addition of **'s** would *look* odd.

- <u>**Descartes'**</u> dreams
- <u>**Camus'**</u> novels

Making Compound Words Possessive

Possessives of compound words are formed in much the same way as with simpler words.

If the compound noun, singular or plural, does not end in <u>s</u>, simply add <u>'s</u>.

GUERRILLA GEEK

If you don't want to worry with whether to add 's or just an apostrophe, think about rewording. For instance, instead of saying
Albert Camus' novels,
Say
The novels of **Albert Camus**.

Singular	Plural
attorney-general	attorney-general's
chief-of-staff	chief-of-staff's
mother-in-law	mother-in-law's

 *To show possession of most common nouns, just add <u>'s</u>.*

The same is true when you have two things jointly showing ownership. No need to give each a separate apostrophe when one will do! Look at these examples:

- <u>**Mary and John's** home</u> was recently redecorated.

This sentence means that there is only one home owned by both Mary and John.

In fact, if you used an apostrophe on each name, something quite different would be conveyed, and you would even need to make other changes in the sentence as well, like making the noun and verb plural.

- <u>Mary's</u> <u>and</u> <u>John's</u> <u>homes</u> <u>were</u> recently redecorated.

Be careful when showing ownership of compound nouns. Pay attention to whether you need one apostrophe for each noun, or just one apostrophe at the end to cover both.

This sentence means that there are two homes: one is Mary's and one is John's.

Here is another example:

- <u>Roger</u> <u>and</u> <u>Marie's</u> <u>son</u> recently graduated from college.

This sentence indicates that Roger and Marie have a son in common, and that he (one person) has just graduated. Compare the meaning of this sentence:

- <u>Roger's</u> <u>and</u> <u>Marie's</u> <u>son</u> recently graduated from college.

GEEKOID

Sometimes company and organization names have more than one part. Put the **'s** after the last part to indicate possession of the entire unit.

- **<u>Gunter, Smith, and Wagner's</u>** annual party will be tonight.
- **<u>Laurel and Hardy's</u>** routines are still funny today.

This change would imply that Roger had a son that graduated, and Marie had a son as well (two separate people).

GEEK
AT A GLANCE

- Nouns can be possessive, that is, they can show ownership.

- Most singular nouns are made possessive simply with the addition of 's.

- When a word already ends in s, there are three options for making it possessive:

  - Just add an apostrophe.
  - Just add 's each time.
  - If the word is singular, add 's; if it is plural, just add the apostrophe.

- No matter which way you choose, be consistent.

- Indicate joint ownership of compound words by adding 's to the last part of the compound. "John and Mary's son came home Friday."

- Indicate individual possessive forms of compounds by adding 's to each part of the compound. "John's and Mary's son came home Friday."

PARDON MY PRONOUN

Pronouns are words that substitute for nouns. They are incredibly useful, and yet they have the distinction of being the most misused of all the parts of speech.

First, before we start to fix problems with pronouns, let's be sure we know what to expect of them. As we've already said, pronouns are understudies for nouns. Being second string might not sound very exciting, but in fact it can keep our sentences from getting repetitive. Think about these sentences.

- **John** is here. **John** is on time. **John** brought **John's** coat with **John**.

As you can tell, it is cumbersome to keep saying John's name. Using pronouns to help, we can say:

- **John** is here. **He** is on time. **He** brought **his** coat with **him**.

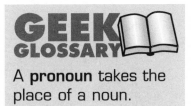

GEEK GLOSSARY

A **pronoun** takes the place of a noun.

Words like **he** and **his** substitute for John so we won't have to keep using his name! We know that they all refer to John without his name being used each time, which would be pretty boring. In grammar terms, the word that you'd have to keep repeating all the time if we didn't use pronouns is called an **antecedent**.

Note another part of this pronoun's job—it has to agree with its antecedent in two important ways: in gender, and in number. That means we have to use **he** if the antecedent is John, and we have to use **she** if the sentence is about Mary. That takes care of the gender part.

It has to agree also in number: If the antecedent is singular, the pronoun has to be singular. If the antecedent is plural, the pronoun has to be, too. This sentence would be incorrect:

- **John** is here. **They** are on time.

An **antecedent** is the word to which your pronoun refers. It is the word you'd have to keep repeating if you didn't have a pronoun to substitute for it.

Why? First of all, your ear will tell you it's not right. It just sounds wrong. But the reason it sounds wrong is because the antecedent is **John** (singular), but the pronoun that replaces his name is **they** (plural). There's only one of John, and he is on time. So the sentence should read this way:

- **John** is here. **He** is on time.

 *This is an important point that bears repeating:* **The pronoun must agree in gender and number with its antecedent.**

Look at this example. It and other similar sentences are heard everyday:

- Each **member** of the class must do **their** own work.

Let's identify the antecedent and pronoun and see if they are working in harmony. The antecedent is <u>member</u>, the pronoun is <u>their</u>. Do they match? No, <u>member</u> is singular, <u>their</u> is plural. Something has to change. We have a couple of options: change the antecedent, or change the pronoun. Here are samples of each:

- Each <u>member</u> must do <u>his</u> or <u>her</u> own work. (Both are singular.)
- <u>Members</u> of the class must do <u>their</u> own work. (Both are plural.)

Now that we know what to expect, we can see that problems with pronouns may happen for two reasons: one is that we're unclear about what word the pronoun is substituting for, and the second is because we choose the wrong pronoun to do the substituting. Let's examine both of those.

<u>Personal</u> <u>pronouns</u> are the most common victims, so we'll begin with those. They are pronouns like <u>I</u>, <u>me</u>, <u>you</u>, <u>him</u>, and <u>her</u> that can take the place of the person speaking (first person), the person being spoken to (second person), or the person being spoken about (third person).

The **number** of a pronoun is literally how many of it there are. If there is only one (he, she, it), the pronoun is singular. If there are more than one (we, they, us), it is plural. The **gender** of a pronoun would be whether it is male or female.

Unclear Reference to Pronoun

Many problems with pronouns happen because we're unclear about which word they're substituting for. Think about this sentence:

- John invited Bob to go bowling because **he** enjoyed it.

Who enjoyed it? It could be either John or Bob. This problem has an easy fix. You could just restate the name that you mean:

- John invited Bob to go bowling because Bob enjoys it.

Or you could completely reword your sentence so that your meaning is clear:

- Because **Bob** enjoys bowling so much, John invited **him** to go with him.
- Because **John** enjoys bowling so much, **he** invited Bob to go with him.

GEEKOID

Plain English Campaign is an independent, self-funded group fighting for public information to be written in plain English. There are more than eight thousand registered supporters in eighty countries. The founder, Chrissie Maher, began her battle for clearer language after seeing two elderly ladies, baffled by a benefits form, die of hypothermia. The campaign was launched as a full-time movement in 1979 by infamously shredding forms in Parliament Square. It is based in New Mills, Derbyshire, England.

Reread your sentences and make sure they say clearly what you intend. A little editing and maybe some rewording should fix any problem with vague pronoun reference.

Case refers to what job function the pronoun is filling at a given time. Pronouns can act as a subject (**subjective case**), an object (**objective case**), or it can show ownership (**possessive case**).

Choosing the Correct Pronoun for the Job

Pronouns have different jobs, and the correct one must be chosen for your need.

Let's talk about the different ways pronouns are used, and then we'll talk about how they're misused. Consider this sentence:

• <u>Sally</u> is a teacher. <u>Sally</u> has three children.

There is no need to keep repeating Sally's name. That's where pronouns come in. We would say

• <u>Sally</u> is a teacher. <u>She</u> has three children.

She is the pronoun that substitutes for **Sally**. In this illustration, it is obvious that **she** refers to **Sally**. This is a simple example. The pronoun is used only in one way. But what about a sentence like:

- **Sally** is a teacher. **Sally** teaches **John**. **Sally** likes **John**.

Using pronouns, we would change this to:

- **Sally** is a teacher. **She** teaches **John**. She likes **him**.

We can see in this example that there are two different pronouns here, **she** and **him**. It is probably obvious, too, that the pronouns are used in different ways: one is the subject that **does** the action, and one is an object that **receives** the action.

As this example shows, pronouns have different jobs. Many people are confused about which pronouns do which jobs. When we talk about the difference in the way they

GUERRILLA GEEK

You may sometimes hear about the **nominative, accusative,** and **genitive** cases. These are just other names for the cases we are already talking about: the nominative or subjective case (used as subjects); the accusative or objective case (used as objects); and the genitive or possessive case (to show possession).

are used, we are talking about their **case**. Our goal will be to learn which pronouns do which job, and make sure we know how to choose the correct ones for each need.

There are basically three cases of pronouns we'll talk about:

- <u>subjective</u> (those used as subjects of sentences)
- <u>objective</u> (those used as objects)
- <u>possessive</u> (those we use to show ownership)

Here is a chart that we'll use in discussing the different job qualifications of pronouns.

JOBS PRONOUNS CAN DO

SINGULAR	SUBJECTS	OBJECTS	POSSESSIVES
1st person	I	me	my, mine
2nd person	you	you	your, yours
3rd person	he, she, it	him, her, it	his, hers, its
PLURAL			
1st person	we	us	our, ours
2nd person	you	you	yours
3rd person	they	them	their, theirs
	who	whom	whose

Subjective Pronouns

Subjective pronouns are used when you need a pronoun for the subject of a sentence. Pronouns used in this way answer the questions "Who?" and "What?".

As you can see from the chart, the subject pronouns are

I	you
he	she
it	we
they	who

Whether you need a singular or plural pronoun, when you need a pronoun for a subject, you will use one of these.

- **She** did not hear us calling the dog.
- **They** left before the game was over.
- **Who** answered the phone when I called?

When you need a pronoun that follows the verb **be** or any of its forms (**am, are, is, was, were, been, being**) use a subject pronoun.

- We discovered the informant to **be** he.
- The most surprised of all **were** he and I.
- Our choice for president **was** she.
- It **is** I.

It's still simple when you have a compound subject. You would still use subject pronouns for both parts of the subject. Note that in the second sentence, your choices for the second part of the subject are presented.

- He bought the book.
- He and (**I**, **me**) bought the book.

If you have trouble deciding which pronoun should be used as the second one, imagine the sentence without the first pronoun. In this case, it would be:

- (**I**, **me**) bought the book.

The correct choice is obviously <u>I</u>, since you would never say, "Me bought the book." You can confirm your correct choice by looking at the chart above, and seeing that the correct subject pronoun is <u>I</u>.

Putting the sentence back together, then, it is correct to say

- <u>He</u> and <u>I</u> bought the book.

 When choosing the second pronoun in a compound pronoun, choose the correct one by imagining the sentence without the first one.

Objective Pronouns

Objective pronouns are those you use as direct objects, indirect objects, and objects of prepositions. They answer the questions, "Whom?" or "What?"

Objective pronouns are these:

me	you
him	her
it	us
them	whom

Insert an objective pronoun when you need a word to receive the action.

- He gave the book to <u>me</u>.
- Give the coupon to <u>her</u>.

Do not be confused by more than one object.

- I gave the package to Sam.
- I gave the package to Sam and (<u>he</u>, <u>him</u>).

Check to see which pronoun you would use by imagining your choice if Sam were not part of the object. In this case it would be,

- I gave the package to (**he**, **him**).

Since the correct choice is obviously **him** (and you can double check that by our chart above), the sentence should now correctly read:

- I gave the package to Sam and **him**.

COMPOUNDING YOUR PRONOUN PROBLEMS

Let's see what happens when you have two choices to make. Let's change that last sentence so that we have to choose two pronouns:

- John gave the package to (**he**, **him**) and (**I**, **me**).

GUERRILLA GEEK

People often incorrectly use **I** as an object, particularly when they are referring to themselves in addition to another person. They think the proper thing is to mention themselves second (which it is), but to always refer to themselves as **I**. You may hear a news commentator, for example, say, "He gave a tour to the officials and I." Now you know that's incorrect. **I** is not used as an object. That sentence should be "He gave a tour to the officials and me."

To make the first choice correctly, you know it wouldn't sound (or be) correct to say "John gave the package to he." So your choice would be <u>him</u>. (See the chart to be sure!) For the second pronoun choice, just pretend that first pronoun isn't there. Imagine the sentence without it: "John gave the package to (<u>I</u>, <u>me</u>)." You can see by the chart that <u>me</u> is the correct choice. Your ear should also know that <u>I</u> doesn't sound right. The correct second choice is <u>me</u>. So now both pronouns are chosen. The sentence should be:

- John gave the package to <u>him</u> and <u>me</u>.

Possessive Pronouns

The possessive pronouns are the ones that show ownership. They answer the question, "Whose?" You can see from the chart that there are specific words we use for that job:

my, mine
our, ours
your, yours
his
her, hers
its, of it
their, theirs
whose

Most people don't have trouble using possessives in general. We usually know how to correctly say, "<u>my</u> dog," or "<u>your</u> cat." But you should be aware that even this simple usage may occur in two different forms: to modify a noun, and as a personal pronoun.

Possessive pronouns that modify nouns are words like <u>my</u>, <u>our</u>, <u>you</u>, <u>your</u>, <u>yours</u>, <u>her</u>, <u>hers</u>, <u>his</u>, <u>its</u>, and <u>their</u>. They answer the question "Whose?" They define the noun: "<u>my</u> cat," "<u>your</u> car," "<u>their</u> party."

Used simply as personal pronouns, to replace a noun, they look like this:

- The shoes are <u>**mine**</u>.
- <u>**Theirs**</u> is the prettiest yard on the street.

There is one possessive pronoun that is chronically misused: <u>its</u>. Note that it has no apostrophe when used correctly. No possessive pronoun ever uses an apostrophe.

Be sure to note that possessive pronouns never have an apostrophe.

- The house on the corner was **their's**. (Incorrect)
- The house on the corner was **theirs**. (Correct)

 Only contractions use apostrophes.

Here is an example of its correct use:

- A puppy wags <u>**its**</u> tail. <u>**It's**</u> cute.

<u>Its</u> is the correct form for showing ownership. It's means "it is." So before you use either one, stop and ask yourself if you mean "It is." If you do, use the contraction. If not, use the one without the apostrophe.

GUERRILLA GEEK

Have you ever heard or even said something like

- "I hope you don't mind **me** going with you"?

We all have. But did you know it's incorrect? Here's why: When you use a **gerund**, an ing word, the pronoun just before it should be possessive. The sentence should correctly be

- I hope you don't mind **my** going with you.

Check these other examples too:

- It was **him** going to the principal that started the problem. [Wrong]
- It was **his** going to the principal that started the problem. [Correct]

- Pronouns substitute for nouns so that nouns do not have to be repeated.

- Pronouns must agree in gender and number with the words to which they refer (the antecedent).

- Be sure you are clear about who or what your antecedent is so you'll know what your pronoun should match.

- Different pronouns are used for different jobs. Choose a subject pronoun for a subject, an object pronoun for an object, and a possessive pronoun to show ownership.

- When using two pronouns in compound subjects or objects, choose the correct second one by imagining how the sentence would sound without the first one.

SOME PRONOUNS I HAVE KNOWN

Even though personal pronouns claim most of the attention, there are other kinds as well. You may never be asked about these, but real geeks want to know!

Reflexive Pronouns

Reflexive pronouns have sometimes been called "mirror" pronouns because they reflect the action of the verb back toward the subject like a mirror. These pronouns are formed using the suffixes –self and –selves to regular personal pronouns to produce words like myself, ourselves, yourself, herself, and himself.

Reflexive pronouns add information by pointing back to a noun or pronoun stated earlier in the sentence.

A good rule to follow is that you should not use these in a sentence unless you have already stated the person to which they refer.

- Give it to John or **myself** when you are finished. (Incorrect)
- **I** will take it **myself** when I go to the office. (Correct)

Reciprocal Pronouns

These are simple pronouns that are often used incorrectly, but they are so easy to correct!

Use **each** **other** when you are talking about two people, two things, etc.

- Clara and Henry helped **each** **other** with the assignment.

Use **one** **another** when you are referring to more than two people or things.

- Mary, Austin, and Harvey helped **one** **another** prepare for the project.

GUERRILLA GEEK

Despite the fact that we often hear them said, there are no such words as **hisself** and **theirselves**. These are nonstandard and are never appropriate to use. These should correctly be expressed as **himself** and **themselves**.

Demonstrative Pronouns

The name of these pronouns makes this a no-brainer: **demonstrative pronouns** demonstrate things! They point things out and identify them. And the way to decide which to use couldn't be easier either: you decide based on how close the objects are!

Reciprocal pronouns show that action is two-way.

<u>This</u> and **these** are used to indicate objects that are close by.

- <u>This</u> is on the best-seller list.
- <u>These</u> go with the purse I bought Friday.

<u>That</u> and **those** are used to indicate objects that are not close by.

GEEK GLOSSARY

Demonstrative pronouns call attention to specific persons, places, or things. They "demonstrate" them.

- <u>That</u> was the bus they took to town.
- <u>Those</u> look like they belong together.

Demonstrative pronouns may also act as adjectives by telling which one, what kind, or how many.

- <u>This</u> meeting is the longest we have had.
- <u>Those</u> children need to learn some manners.

Relative Pronouns

<u>Relative</u> <u>pronouns</u> relate parts of the same sentence to each other. They substitute for nouns, relating appropriately to its antecedent and joining it to words that help complete it. Examples of this type of pronoun include <u>where</u>, <u>when</u>, <u>why</u>, and <u>what</u>. Let's look at some examples to see how they function.

GEEK*Speak:*

"I try to write down every word with caution and a sense of craft, as though I were carving hieroglyphics on the tomb of a well-loved king."

Pat Conroy

- You did <u>what</u> you were told.
- This is the house <u>where</u> I grew up.
- We are leaving <u>when</u> the program is over.

This group also includes some that have been known to be real troublemakers: <u>that</u>, <u>which</u>, <u>who</u>, and <u>whom</u>. But they needn't be a problem. Let's see how we can master those relative pronouns that sometimes cause confusion.

GEEK GLOSSARY

Relative pronouns relate one part of the sentence to another.

- **Who/whom** — There's no need to be confused about the use of **who** and **whom**. Use **who** when you need a subject pronoun, and **whom** when you need an object. **Who** tells who did the action, **whom** tells who receives the action.

A good way to double-check your choice of <u>who</u> or <u>whom</u> is to mentally replace them each in your sentence with <u>he</u> or <u>him</u>. If you find that <u>he</u> works, you need a subject pronoun and so your choice would be <u>who</u>. If <u>him</u> is a better fit, use <u>whom</u>.

As an example, look at this sentence:

- (<u>Who</u>, <u>Whom</u>) took the key to the cabinet?

Mentally fill in that choice with <u>He</u>, and you have "He took the key to the cabinet." That sounds right, but just to be sure, let's see what <u>Him</u> would sound like: "Him took the key to the cabinet." Nope! <u>He</u> has to be

GEEK Speak:

"The limits of my language mean the limits of my world."
Ludwig Wittgenstein

the choice, which means you need a subject pronoun, and <u>Who</u> is the pronoun for that job!

- <u>Who</u> took the key to the cabinet?

Let's try another one:

- (<u>Who</u>, <u>Whom</u>) should we charge for the printing?

In your mind, think whether <u>he</u> or <u>him</u> could be inserted instead of <u>who</u> or <u>whom</u>. Let's change the order of the words just a little to help us:

- We should charge <u>he</u> for the printing.

That doesn't sound right. Let's try <u>him</u>.

- We should charge <u>him</u> for the printing.

That's it! And that means we need an object pronoun, so the correct choice is <u>whom</u>.

<u>Whom</u> should we charge for the printing?

 *Use **who** when you need a subject pronoun, and **whom** wen you need an object pronoun.*

That/which — We very often interchange these without giving them much thought, but actually, they do have different functions. Use **that** to introduce words that are essential to the meaning of the sentence. Use **which** to introduce non-essential phrases.

45

GEEKOID

Using pronouns for comparison and can't decide which to use in a sentence like this?
    He is older than (**I**, **me**).

Expand the sentence in your mind, and use the choice that sounds best then.
    He is older than (**I**, **me**) [am].

The correct choice is obvious:
    He is older than **I**.

- The meeting **that** I attended was very helpful.

"**That I attended**" is an essential part of the sentence because it specifies what meeting you mean, so **that** is the appropriate word to introduce it. Do not use commas with it.

- The report on the event, **which** I sent you last week, should be enlightening.

"**Which I sent you last week**" is not essential to the sentence. It may be interesting, but the sentence would be fine without it, so it is set off by commas.

 *Use **that** to introduce words that are essential to the sentence. Use **which** to introduce non-essential phrases set off by commas.*

Gender Pronouns

Even though we should make all efforts to have the **gender** of a pronoun agree with its antecedent, there are times when you will want to avoid mention of a specific gender. Particularly if you write in your work, there are times when reference to a particular gender might be regarded as sexist. More and more, people are opting for gender-free writing and speaking. This can easily be done by careful word selection.

Instead of	Use
Businessman/woman	Businessperson
Chairman/woman	Chairperson
Waiter/waitress	Server

- Reflexive pronouns direct action back to the subject.

- Reciprocal pronouns show action between two things.

- Demonstrative pronouns point out items.

- Relative pronouns show relations of words to each other.

THE VIVACITY OF VERBS

Verbs show action or state of being. That means that some tell what the subject is doing, and some tell how the subject is being.

Every sentence needs a verb. You might have a sentence without a stated subject, but you can never have a sentence without a verb!

Some verbs tell what action you're doing (I **talk** on the phone every night.), and that's why they're called <u>action</u> <u>verbs</u>. Others that express a state of being or what condition you are in (I **am** miserable.) are called <u>linking</u> <u>verbs</u>.

Verbs are the most important part of a sentence. But they take directions from the subject.

Even though verbs are the most critical part of the sentence, they take their cue from the subject, no matter if the subject is a noun(s) or pronoun(s). We have to know the subject before we can know the proper verb to use. Like any other good partners, they must agree.

Identifying the Subject

Let's be sure we know how to identify the subject of a sentence. Look at this example.

- Joanie took the dog home.

It is easy to see in this example that Joanie is the subject. She does the action. But what about this example?

- One of the boys on the team is my brother.

It's tempting to think that either <u>boys</u> or <u>team</u> might be the subject because they look like good, solid nouns, but they're not the subject. They're serving right now as objects. We know that because they follow prepositions, so they are the objects of prepositions. That leaves the word <u>One</u> as the subject of the sentence. Since that word is obviously singular, the correct verb is <u>is</u>.

GEEKOID

Some action verbs depict action that you can observe, like **move**, **jump**, and **write**. Other action verbs describe unseen action, like **think**, or **appreciate**.

That brings us to an important point: do not be confused by extra words that seem to be a part of your subject. Eliminate them as you identify your subject. As the example above shows, sometimes there are prepositional phrases that are closer to the verb than its own subject, and we get confused about the subject in those cases.

Take a look at this example and see if it has the correct verb.

- A quartet of girls were entered in the contest.

If you think the sentence is correct, you may not have correctly identified the subject! It is easy to think that the subject is <u>girls</u> and that the verb for it is correct.

But that's not true. <u>Girls</u> is serving here as an object of the preposition **of**, so it cannot be the subject. Cross that out mentally, and you see that the subject is <u>quartet</u>. It is a collective noun that needs **was** for its verb. The sentence should correctly be written as:

- A <u>quartet</u> of girls <u>was</u> entered in the contest.

GEEKOID

Real geeks won't be fooled by extra words that surround the true subject. Mentally cross those out and identify the real subject so you'll know whether you need a singular or a plural verb.

Agreement of Subject and Verb

Since we now know how to identify a subject, we can know how to make a verb agree with it.

 *If the subject is singular, the verb must be appropriately singular. Likewise for plural subject/verb pairs.*

Consider this sentence:

- The building <u>sways</u> in high winds.

GEEKOID

To help you decide the correct subject/verb combination, imagine a shortage of the letter **s**. The **s** must be rationed, so you can give it to either the subject OR the verb, but not both. This will usually help your subject and verb agree.

- The **member has** a new card.
- The **members have** a new card.

- The **girl jumps** rope.
- The **girls jump** rope.

When the subject is made plural, the verb must change too.

- The buildings <u>sway</u> in high winds.

Choosing Verbs for Compound Subjects

What if the subject is <u>compound</u> (having more than one), as in this sentence?

GUERRILLA GEEK

Here's another way to be sure you use the correct verb. In your imagination, put a pronoun in the place of the subject. In this case, the correct pronoun would be **it** when you mean one building; and **they** when you mean more buildings. Now think about the sentence with these pronouns as the subjects. The verb choices are easy now:

- **It sways** in high winds.
- **They sway** in high winds.

- <u>Alice</u> and <u>Mary</u> are the team's leaders.
- <u>Swimming</u> and <u>reading</u> <u>are</u> my favorite hobbies.

Obviously, these subjects are plural because they are joined by <u>and</u>, so <u>are</u> is an easy choice for a plural verb in each case.

If the parts of the compound subject are joined by <u>or</u>, use a singular verb.

- John, Martha, <u>or</u> Beatrice <u>is</u> going to represent our office.

If your subject is expressed in dollars, use a singular verb when a specific sum of money is mentioned. Use plural for general amounts.
- Twenty dollars is too much to pay for lunch. (Specific amount)
- Millions of dollars are needed to repair the damage. (General amount)

If the parts are all plural, even if they are joined by <u>or</u>, use a plural subject.

- Dogs, cats, <u>or</u> hamsters <u>make</u> the best pets.

But what if one part of the compound subject is singular, and one part is plural?

- John or the boys <u>want</u> to stop for the night.

When choosing a verb for a compound subject, if one subject is singular and one is plural, choose a verb appropriate for the closest subject.

GEEKOID

Sometimes, verbs need a little help from their friends to get the job done. To show different tenses of verbs, the primary verb may be joined by a helper verb. Common helpers are words like **have**, **had**, **will**, **would**, **could**, **may**, **might**, and **must**. These usually help to identify whether the action is current, past, or future.

- I **will go** before it is too late.
- Susan **could be** available to help if needed.

In this case, make the verb agree with the subject nearer to it. <u>Boys</u> is nearer to the verb, so those two elements must agree.

Moody Verbs

You wouldn't think such an important part of speech would be moody, but verbs are. Luckily, their moods are limited to just three: <u>indicative</u>, <u>imperative</u>, and <u>subjunctive</u>.

The <u>indicative mood</u> is used to state a fact, ask a question, or make an exclamation. This is the most commonly used mood in the English language. Here are some examples.

- I saw my friend at school yesterday.

GEEK GLOSSARY

The **mood** of a verb is the manner in which the action or condition is conceived or intended. It refers to the attitude that a writer or speaker has to what is being written or spoken.

GUERRILLA GEEK

Verbals are words that start out as verbs, but later become other parts of speech. There are three types: infinitives, gerunds, and participles.

Infinitives are made of the word **to**, plus a verb: **to go, to write, to begin**. The infinitive may be used as a noun, as in this sentence, where it is the subject: **To read** has always been by favorite pastime.

Gerunds are verbs to which **ing** has been added, also making them nouns. In this sentence, the gerund is the object of the verb. His favorite sport was **running**.

Participles are verb forms that act as adjectives. They also end with **ing** and sometimes **ed**, and modify nouns or pronouns. An example would be: The **stomped** ash was quickly extinguished.

- What did you do after the party?
- Our team won!

The <u>imperative</u> <u>mood</u> is used to make commands, polite requests, or to give directions. You don't usually state a subject in sentences with the imperative mood, but the subject "you" is always implied.

- Raise that window and let some air in.

- Clean the chalkboard before you leave.
- Please, take your brother with you.

The **subjunctive mood** indicates statements that are contrary to fact. They very often begin with "If." There are actually two different ways to handle the subjunctive. If you are making a statement that is not now true, and is not likely to be at any time, use the verb **were**.

GEEK*Speak:*

"Language is the means of getting an idea from my brain into yours without surgery."
Mark Amidon

GUERRILLA GEEK

The rule about infinitives, such as **to study**, and to understand, says that you shouldn't split them, that is, put words between to and the verb.

They wanted to quickly run to the grocery store.

People mostly disregard that now. . .ever hear of "To boldly go..."? Sometimes you can end up with a more awkward sentence trying to be perfectly correct than just giving in and splitting it. So you decide. Do you want to be perfectly correct, or write in a more conversational tone? This choice is up to you.

GEEKOID

Some verbs just always give us trouble. Here are a couple that we use a lot, and how we can use them correctly.

- **Set** – indicates motion and placing something: "Set the vase there."
- **Sit** – indicates position in place: "Sit there until time to go."

- **Lay** – indicates motion and placing something: "Lay the book on the table."
- **Lie** – indicates being at rest: "I will lie here for a brief nap."

- If I <u>were</u> rich, I would buy you all presents.
- If she <u>were</u> better prepared, the test would be easy.

For statements that might actually be true, use <u>was</u>.

- If I <u>was</u> rude to you just now, I apologize.
- If I <u>was</u> talking out of turn, forget what I said.

- Action verbs describe action. Linking verbs describe a state of being.

- Subjects and verbs must agree with each other. Singular subjects must have singular verbs. Plural subjects need plural verbs.

- Compound subjects are plural and need plural verbs.

- The mood of a verb indicates the manner in which the verb is expressed. The indicative mood simply makes statements. The imperative mood gives commands. The subjunctive mood makes statements contrary to actual facts.

- An infinitive is the word <u>to</u> plus a verb form such as <u>to go</u>. A split infinitive occurs when a descriptive word is put in between these two words.

DEFINING MOMENTS OF ADJECTIVES

Adjectives are words that describe nouns and pronouns. They dress them up. They tell which one, what kind, how many, or to what extent.

When you go to your favorite restaurant and see a mouth-watering description of all the dishes available, thank an adjective! For instance, which would you be more likely to order?

A hamburger

OR

A <u>sizzling</u>, <u>juicy</u>, <u>flame-broiled</u>, <u>cheese-topped</u> hamburger?

Of course the second one sounds better, and it's because of adjectives.

GEEK GLOSSARY

Adjectives describe nouns and pronouns by telling which one, what kind, how many, and to what extent.

Adjectives add color to language by providing descriptive details.

Most adjectives are easy to identify.

- The <u>big</u> tree created a <u>wonderful </u>shade for us.
- Mom gave candy to the <u>three</u> <u>little </u>boys.

The adjectives are easy to find here because they are right next to the words they modify.

But don't always count on finding them positioned this way. Look at this example.

- The pianist we heard at the concert was <u>brilliant</u>.

In this sentence, the adjective and the word it describes are at opposite ends of the sentence.

In grammar, **modify** means to describe or define. By giving more details about nouns and pronouns, adjectives **modify** them. Since that's their job description, their job title is **modifier**.

Three Little Words: Articles

Probably the most widely recognized adjectives are <u>a</u>, <u>an</u>, and <u>the</u>. These three little words are called <u>**articles**</u>. One of the three of these usually introduces each noun or pronoun.

We seldom have trouble knowing when to use <u>the</u>, but we do sometimes have a problem knowing whether to use <u>a</u> or <u>an</u>.

Here is a general rule for knowing whether to use <u>a</u> or <u>an</u>:

Use <u>a</u> before words beginning with consonant *sounds*.

- <u>a</u> boy
- <u>a</u> girl
- <u>a</u> dish

Be sure to note that it's consonant <u>sounds</u>, but it does not have to be words beginning with actual consonants. They only have to sound

Article adjectives are **a**, **an**, and **the**.

that way. Here are some words that begin with vowels, but sound like they begin with consonants.

- **a** one o-clock class (one sounds like it begins with w)
- **a** unique opportunity

When referring to something specific, use **the**. *Use* **a** *or* **an** *for general references.*

Use **an** before words beginning with vowel *sounds*.

- **an** apple
- **an** owl
- **an** energy source

GEEKOID

The most commonly used word in written English is **the**, but the most commonly spoken word is **I**, followed, in order, by **you**, **the**, and **a**.

There are some words that begin with consonants, but sound like they begin with vowels. These should be preceded by <u>an</u>.

- <u>an</u> honor (the h is silent; you hear the o)
- <u>an</u> M.D. (M sounds like it begins with EM)

*Remember that it is the sound of the word being described that determines whether you use **a** or **an**. Use **a** before a consonant **sound**, and **an** before a vowel **sound**.*

Comparative Adjectives

Adjectives are great for comparison.

We can take an adjective like <u>sweet</u>, and can usually add <u>er</u> or <u>est</u> to show comparison between two and three items.

GEEKOID

If you have two nouns, one beginning with a vowel sound, and one with a consonant sound, use two separate articles.

They want to choose **a** lawyer and **an** accountant.

If you try to make one article do for both, the meaning of your sentence will not be clear.

They want to choose **a** lawyer and accountant.

That sounds like they want one person qualified to be an expert in two professions.

Adjective	Comparison of two things	Comparison of three things
sweet	sweeter	sweetest

Here are some other examples of comparative words.

Adjective	Comparative Degree	Superlative Degree
pretty	prettier	prettiest
tall	taller	tallest
young	younger	youngest

When you compare two things, you are using the **comparative degree**; *when you compare three or more, you are using the* **superlative degree***.*

Here's how those comparative forms are used in sentences:

GEEK GLOSSARY

An **adnoun** is the use of an adjective as a noun. An example would be this sentence: **Blessed are the merciful**.

- She is a **pretty** woman. (simple adjective describing a noun)
- She is **prettier** than her friend. (comparison of two things – comparative)
- She is the **prettiest** of all her friends. (comparison of more than two – superlative)

Some adjectives can be used for comparison just by adding **er** *or* **est** *to their basic form. But some require helper words like* **more** *and* **most***.*

GUERRILLA GEEK

Fewer and **less** are comparative words that are often confused with each other. Here's how to know which to use:

Fewer usually refers to a small, manageable number. It is used with plural nouns.

Fewer drivers than normal tried the hazardous path.

Less refers to a more general amount, and is used with singular nouns.

We had **less paper** on hand than we thought.

For some adjectives, just adding <u>er</u> and <u>est</u> isn't enough. You will need to add the words more and most before the adjective.

<u>Adjective</u>	<u>Comparative Degree</u>	<u>Superlative Degree</u>
capable	more capable	most capable
reasonable	more reasonable	most reasonable

Some grammarians say the way to decide whether to use er/est comparisons, or the more/most comparisons, is to use the former for shorter words, the latter for longer words. Consult a good dictionary if you are unsure. But do not use both methods at the same time.

 *Some adjectives follow no set patterns when making comparisons.*

Also realize that there are some comparative words that do not simply add **er** or **est** to a root word. For these exceptions, there is a different word for each comparison.

Adjective	Comparative form	Superlative form
good	better	best
many	more	most

Compound Adjectives

Sometimes a combination of words is needed to describe something, and these are called **compound adjectives**. They are usually considered to be a single unit, and when they come right before the noun, they should be hyphenated.

- The **point-of-sale** terminals were installed Monday.

Look at the compound adjective and see how the words depend upon each other. Alone, none would adequately describe the terminals.

GUERRILLA GEEK

Do not use comparative forms for words that cannot logically be compared—for example, words like pregnant. There are stages of being pregnant, but either you are, or you aren't; there are not degrees of it. Other words that have no degrees include unique, dead, impossible, and perfect (with all due respect to our Founding Fathers, who wrote of forming "a more perfect union"). You may, however, precede these with qualifier words like "almost" or "nearly."

Adjective Pronouns

Remember the demonstrative pronouns we talked about earlier: this, that, these, those? Sometimes they can also work as adjectives by modifying nouns and other pronouns. When used like this, these pronouns tell which one, what kind, how many, or to what extent, just like regular adjectives. Here are some examples of this use.

- **This** book is on the list of required reading.
- **That** boy is the one who played in the recital.
- **These** shoes go with my new dress.
- **Those** gloves were left on the church pew.

- Adjectives describe nouns and pronouns.

- There are three adjectives called articles: a, an, and the.

- Adjectives help compare people and things: sweet, sweeter, sweetest.

- Some adjectives need helper words to make comparisons: reliable, more reliable, most reliable.

- Some comparative words follow no set pattern: good, better, best.

THEY'RE NOT CALLED ADVERBS FOR NOTHING

Adverbs also describe, but they tell about verbs. They do just what their name says: they ADD to VERBS = ADVERBS. They tell when, where, how, why, or to what extent something happened.

Adverbs give us more information about what action is happening. Here's how they look in a sentence.

- We ran <u>quickly</u> to get out of the rain.
- The car rolled <u>slowly</u> as it ran out of gas.

GEEKOID

Like adjectives, adverbs do not have to be next to the word they're modifying.

 *You can almost always recognize an adverb because they usually end in **ly**.*

But don't take adverbs for granted! They don't always end in <u>ly</u>, and they don't always just modify (describe) verbs, either. Sometimes they tell you more about adjectives and other adverbs. Here are some examples.

GEEKOID

Adverbs add to verbs, but they also describe adjectives and other adverbs as well.

Monday was a **very beautiful** day.
(The adverb **very** modifies the adjective **beautiful**.)

Seth pitched the ball **quite slowly**.
(The adverb **quite** modifies the adverb **slowly**.)

Erwin has a **badly injured** knee.
(The adverb **badly** modifies the adjective **injured**.)

Comparative Adverbs

Like adjectives, adverbs can be used to compare things by adding <u>er</u> or <u>est</u>. The <u>er</u> form compares two things, the <u>est</u> form compares three or more things.

Adverb	Comparative Degree	Superlative Degree
new	newer	newest
fast	faster	fastest

- My car went <u>fast</u>.
- My car went <u>faster</u> than his.
- My car went the <u>fastest</u> of all of them.

Like adjectives, some adverbs take booster words, too.

Adverb	Comparative Degree	Superlative Degree
coldly	more coldly	most coldly
lovely	more lovely	most lovely

- The judge stared **coldly** at the prisoner.
- The judge stared **more** **coldly** at his accomplice.
- The judge stared **most** **coldly** at the hardened criminal.

Problem Adverbs

With all the jobs adverbs do for us, they're not without their problems. Here are a few that are chronic offenders.

GEEK*Speak:*

"Shall I compare thee to a summer's day? Thou art more lovely and more temperate."
William Shakespeare

WELL/GOOD

Many people use the words **good** and **well** interchangeably, but they actually have different jobs. **Well** is actually the adverb. It helps tell more about a verb. **Good** is an adjective that describes a noun. Look at the difference in function of these two words in similar sentences.

- I do my job **well**. (**Well** describes the verb. It tells how you do the job.)
- I have a **good** job. (**Good** tells about the noun. It tells the kind of job you have.)

REALLY

This word causes problems only because it is overused. People use it almost without thinking to emphasize other descriptive words: really well or really slowly. While it is not incorrect, using the word <u>really</u> is a lazy choice. Try to find something else to use for the sake of variety.

Weak sentence:
- It was a <u>**really**</u> good game.

Better sentences:
- It was an <u>**exciting**</u> game.
- It was a <u>**fast-paced**</u> game.
- It was a <u>**surprising**</u> game.

GEEK*Speak:*

"Rather, very, little, pretty—these are the leeches that infest the pond of prose, sucking the blood of words."
                E.B. White

HARDLY/SCARCELY/BARELY

These are negative words, and only one should be used at a time. If you use two, you have created a double negative, and you cancel out what you intended to say. Consider the difference in these two sentences:

- He <u>**hardly**</u> had time to get his work done.

This means that he did not have time to get his work done. If you have two negatives, it looks like this:

- He <u>**didn't**</u> <u>**hardly**</u> have time to get his work done.

If you take time to see what this really says, it means he didn't not have time, which means he did have time.

GEEK AT A GLANCE

- Adverbs describe verbs, adjectives, and other adverbs.

- Adverbs help to make comparisons: new, newer, newest.

- Some adverbs need helper words to make comparisons: calmly, more calmly, most calmly.

AROUND AND ABOUT PREPOSITIONS

Prepositions are words that show the relation of one thing to another.

Prepositions are the perfect example of little things that come in small packages.

Examples of prepositions include words like <u>on</u>, <u>above</u>, <u>in</u>, <u>around</u>, <u>through</u>, and <u>near</u>. Many, but not all, prepositions, are small words. You'd recognize them as words like <u>at</u>, <u>for</u>, <u>in</u>, and <u>to</u>. But they also include words like <u>about</u>, <u>after</u>, <u>among</u>, <u>before</u>, <u>beside</u>, <u>between</u>, <u>over</u>, <u>through</u>, and <u>under</u>.

Prepositions are words that show relation between other words.

These words wouldn't be very useful alone. They rely on their objects, or words that complete their thought, to bring meaning to their jobs. It wouldn't be much use to say "on" if you didn't say on what. Or "near" if you didn't say near what. So prepositional phrases look like this:

Prepositions must have **objects** to complete their meanings.

- <u>by</u> the tree (by is the preposition; tree is the object)
- <u>with</u> his sister (with is the preposition; sister is the object)
- <u>under</u> the table (under is the preposition; table is the object)

Prepositions rely on their objects to define their meaning.

We have already mentioned in a previous chapter that it's important to recognize prepositions and their objects so we don't confuse them with other things in a sentence. In particular, sometimes they are confused with the subject of the sentence, and mislead us into choosing an incorrect verb.

As a quick review, look at this sentence.

• One of the members says "No" to the proposal.

In order to know the correct verb to use, you have to identify the subject of the sentence. Do not let the prepositional phrase confuse you into thinking that **members** is the subject, and that the verb should be **say**. Recognize **of the members** as a prepositional

GUERRILLA GEEK

Don't make the cure worse than the disease. Despite what most people think, it is acceptable to end a sentence with a preposition. There are no rules that prohibit it, and efforts to avoid it usually produce an awkward result. Just make sure if you end with a preposition, it's one that's really needed. In the sentence, "Where is she at?" the final word should be omitted not because it's a preposition, but because it is simply not needed. The sentence would be correct written as "Where is she?"

phrase and know that it cannot be your subject. Mentally cross it out. Now it is obvious that your subject is **One**, and that your verb should be **says**.

 *Do not confuse prepositional phrases with your subject. Be sure you can identify your subject by first eliminating prepositional phrases.*

It is possible that a prepositional phrase may *sometimes* be the subject, as in this example.

• **For us to leave now** is unthinkable.

But if there's a noun or pronoun nearby, one of those is most likely the subject.

Problem Prepositions

Almost every part of speech has some trouble-makers you need to watch out for, and prepositions are no exception. Here are a few with which you'll need to be especially careful.

AMONG/BETWEEN

These two words are both prepositions, but they have particular uses. Knowing which one to use when can set you apart as being someone who knows the finer points of grammar.

Among indicates comparison of three or more things. **Between** is a word used when you are comparing only two things.

• **Among** the people in that office, Joe had the most seniority.
• **Between** the **two** of us, Mary has worked here longer.

IN/INTO

The difference between these two words is small, but significant if you are to know and use grammar correctly. **Into** indicates movement. **In** indicates a position inside something.

GEEK*Speak:*

"Ending a sentence with a preposition is something up with which I will not put."
Winston Churchill

- The file is <u>in</u> the cabinet.
- Move the table for the demonstration <u>into</u> the meeting room.

GEEK AT A GLANCE

- Prepositions show the relation of one thing to another: on the stove, in the box.

- Ending a sentence with a preposition is acceptable according to certain standard grammar usage. Ending with a preposition is usually preferable to the awkward sentence that results from efforts to write "correctly."

BEING WELL CONNECTED WITH CONJUNCTIONS

Conjunctions are connecting words. They are used to join related thoughts and ideas. They help offer a smooth flow of words and ideas.

This part of speech includes common joining words like **and** and **but**. But conjunctions also include words like **for**, **yet**, and **so**. They help to make a transition from one group of words to another.

Coordinating Conjunctions

This basic form of conjunctions looks like this, joining two related things or ideas.

- The dog **and** the cat stood by the door.

Conjunctions can also join two related complete thoughts.

- The dog **and** the cat stood by the door, **and** I finally let them in.

GEEK GLOSSARY

Conjunctions are words that connect related ideas.

Subordinating Conjunctions

Some conjunctions are used to join lesser important (subordinate), but supporting, parts of a sentence, to the main part. These are called **subordinating** **conjunctions**. These are words like **although**, **as**, **because**, **even though**, **though**, **since**, **whereas**, and **while**. They work like this.

Common conjunctions are **and**, **but**, and **or**. But other words, such as **nor**, **for**, **yet**, and **so** may also help join thoughts.

- It was raining, **so** the game was postponed.
- James didn't ask me to go, **nor** did I want him to.

- **Although** I told him to be prompt, Jack was late for the meeting.
- I took the car **because** it was too far to walk.
- Janet left the meeting early **since** she had another appointment.

Correlative Conjunctions

GEEK GLOSSARY

Coordinating conjunctions join related ideas.

Be aware that some conjunctions must be used in pairs. These are called **correlative** **conjunctions**, and include words like:

- both…and
- either…or
- neither…nor
- not only…but also

All words in the pairs must be used to work properly.

- Denise is **not only** beautiful **but** smart. (Incorrect)
- Denise is **not only** beautiful **but also** smart. (Correct)

Here are some other examples of correct usage:

GUERRILLA GEEK

Just like the "rule" that says you can't end a sentence with a preposition, there's another "rule" that says you can't begin a sentence with a conjunction. That's not so! You can begin with a conjunction, just don't do it too often.

- **Both** the teacher **and** the principal met with the parents. (Correct)
- **Either** Spanish **or** Band may be taken as an elective. (Correct)
- **Neither** the boys **nor** the girls were in the majority. (Correct)

 *When a singular and a plural subject are joined by one of these pairs, the verb will agree with the subject closest to it.*

GEEK GLOSSARY

Correlative conjunctions come in pairs. For these to completely do their jobs, all parts of each pair should be present.

- **Neither** the principal **nor** the teachers **was** there. (Incorrect)
- **Neither** the principal **nor** the teachers **were** at the meeting. (Correct)
- **Neither** the teachers **nor** the principal **was** at the meeting. (Correct)

Conjunctive Adverbs

Sometimes, adverbs can be used to join two independent thoughts. They're still adverbs, but they just act like conjunctions in particular cases.

Some of the words that can help make transitions like this include <u>accordingly</u>, <u>afterwards</u>, <u>consequently</u>, <u>however</u>, <u>indeed</u>, <u>likewise</u>, <u>moreover</u>, <u>nevertheless</u>, <u>nonetheless</u>, <u>otherwise</u>, <u>still</u>, and <u>therefore</u>

Conjunctive adverbs function as conjunctions by joining two independent thoughts.

Here are some examples of how these temporary conjunctions work.

- The teacher will attend the meeting; **accordingly**, she will have a substitute in charge of her class.
- I bought my dress before the sale; **consequently**, I paid full price.

Choosing the Correct Conjunction

Once we know the job of different conjunctions, and how to recognize them, we must recognize how important it is to use just the right word for the meaning you intend. Notice the difference in these similar sentences.

- The meeting was long **and** interesting.

In this sentence, we might think that the meeting was interesting in spite of being long.

- The meeting was long **but** interesting.

But in this sentence, we might think that the meeting was interesting despite the fact that it was long.

GUERRILLA GEEK

Elements joined by the conjunctions should be expressed in the same way, that is, they should be parallel.

I like both **singing** and to **dance**. (Incorrect)

I like both **singing** and **dancing**. (Correct)

Note that in this example, both parts share a verb. What if each part has its own verb? In that case, make sure that each verb follows its conjunctive word.

Esther **not only makes** refreshments **but also decorates** for the party.

There are other more formal words that join thoughts, like **therefore**, **nevertheless**, and **however**. See the difference you can make in your sentences by using just the right one.

- Jean studied music at the Academy; **therefore**, he played well.

The use of the word therefore indicates that Jean played well because he studied at the Academy. But look at the difference in the sentence when we use a different conjunction.

- Jean studied music at the Academy; **nevertheless**, he played well.

Using the word **nevertheless** makes you think that he played well in spite of having studied at the Academy.

Use **nevertheless** when the sentence offers a conclusion that is different than you might have expected.

GEEK *Speak:*

"All the words I use in my stories can be found in the dictionary—it's just a matter of arranging them into the right sentences."

Somerset Maugham

- Conjunctions join related words.

- There are several types of conjunctions: coordinating, subordinating, correlative, and conjunctive adverbs.

- Correlative conjunctions used in pairs must have all parts of the pairs present for correct use.

- When singular and plural words are joined by a conjunctive pair, the following verb must agree with the subject closer to it.

- Elements joined by conjunctions should be expressed in similar (parallel) ways.

ALL "I'S" ON INTERJECTIONS

Interjections are words that show strong emotion. They often begin the sentence and are usually just one or two words.

Interjections are usually easy to identify because they are generally followed by an exclamation point, though sometimes even a comma will do. Here are some examples:

- Well!
- Oh boy!
- Well, take that attitude then.

Here are some descriptions you may not know about interjections:

Independent — Even though they often introduce a thought, interjections are not grammatically part of a sentence. Take for example, this sentence:

- "Whew! What a long letter we received from Judy."

GEEK GLOSSARY

Interjections show strong emotion and are usually followed by an exclamation point. They serve no grammatical purpose, and are only included to add emotion.

The word <u>whew</u> is not essential to any other part of the sentence, and you could even delete it without changing the meaning of the main thought.

Intense — Interjections show strong emotion. With spoken language, there is no problem in identifying interjections. But with written language, strong feelings are followed by exclamation points.

- Wow! What a race we saw.
- Ouch! That hurt!

GEEKOID

Even though the primary job of interjections is to show emotion, they have quite a big job to do. With just one word, this uncommon part of speech must show feelings like surprise, dismay, disappointment, fear, annoyance, confusion, and pain, just to name a few.

Interesting — Interjections actually have a dual personality. One part is made of interjections that cannot be any other part of speech. These would include words like Ouch! The other part of their personality lets them act as other parts of speech, too. An example would be a word like What!

GEEKOID

Some grammarians even consider the word **like** to be an interjection when it is used this way: **"Like, I'm so sure!"**

- Interjections show strong emotion.

- They usually introduce a sentence, but are not connected to it grammatically.

- Interjections may be followed by an exclamation point, or even a comma.

POINTERS FOR PERFECT PUNCTUATION

When you speak directly with people, they have the benefit of seeing your facial expressions, and of hearing your voice rise to imply a question, or fall to indicate that you have finished a statement.

When people read your words, however, they do not have that advantage. So you need some system to indicate such things as where the pauses are, where a thought is indicated, or when you're about to give a list of things. Those jobs and more are what good punctuation will do. It will serve as road signs to help your reader understand more clearly what you mean by the words you have used.

Think of good punctuation as a code that you and your reader have agreed upon to help you understand each other.

THE POINT OF PERIODS

Periods (.) are the punctuation mark that we're most familiar with because most of our sentences end with this form of punctuation.

Despite its popularity, the period is ranked by many experts as second to the comma in terms of use. At any rate, there are times when only a period will do.

The primary use of a period is to signal the end of a declarative or imperative sentence.

- We went to dinner after the game. (Declarative)
- Take that pot off the stove before it boils. (Imperative)

The earliest work on punctuation is the anonymous *Treatise of Stops, Points, or Pauses,* published in London in 1680. It presented the theory of punctuation as being based entirely on breathing and rhetorical pauses.

The period shows that you have completed your thought.

A period is also appropriate at the end of an indirect question—this is when someone is asking for information, and expecting it, but it is not really put in the form of a direct question.

- He asked when I could start to work.
- Mary wanted to know why I wasn't able to finish the work on time.

GEEKOID

Jeff Rubin founded National Punctuation Day® to remind students of the importance of proper punctuation, and to stress to businesspeople that they are often judged professionally by how they present themselves in writing. The day was originally celebrated in August, but its permanent date will be September 24 so students can get in on the action during their school year.

There are also statements that in effect make a request, and yet they are made as a simple statement of fact. These are called polite requests.

- Will you please let me know when you are available.
- May I please have a prompt response to my inquiry.

 *Periods are used to conclude a polite request— a request made as a simple statement of fact.*

Periods are used after standard abbreviations:

- Dr., Mr., Mrs., Rev., i.e.

They should not, however, be used after a contraction.

- do not   don't
- will not   won't

Periods should also be used in outlines and lists. When items are numbered or lettered, the numbers and letters are followed by a period. The items listed should begin with a capital letter. Note that no period is used after the items.

Types of Pronouns
1. Personal
2. Reflexive
3. Demonstrative
4. Relative

Longer items may be presented in a vertical list. The items carry no closing punctuation unless they consist of a complete sentence. When the list is introduced by a complete sentence, items begin with a lowercase letter, semicolons may be used between items, and the final item is followed by a period.

GEEKOID

British practices usually do not include periods after such common abbreviations as Mr. and Mrs., but if you omit them in the good ol' USA, it will look like an error. By the way, in Britain, the period is called a **full stop**.

The job was handled by a local company that
1. knew the territory;
2. was familiar with the employees;
3. had time to devote to it.

Sometimes, periods are used alongside other forms of punctuation. Here's what to do then.

When used with quotation marks, periods go inside closing quotation marks. This won't always look right, but that is the proper way to do it in the United States.

GEEK🔍OID

Do not use a period following an **acronym** (a word formed from the initial letters of words of a name). For instance, NASA (National Aeronautics and Space Administration) is written without periods.

Here's an example:

- I wanted to read the chapter on "Pardon My Pronoun."

Written by itself, the chapter title "Pardon My Pronoun" would not include any punctuation at all within the quotation marks, particularly not a period. So you might wonder why the period that ends the entire sentence would be included in quotations with the title of the chapter. "Because standard American English says so" is the only answer I can give. It is correct because it is. Periods go inside quotation marks.

GEEK AT A GLANCE

- Periods follow declarative sentences.

- Periods also follow polite requests.

- In standard American usage, periods follow standard abbreviations, but are not used after acronyms.

- When periods are used with quotation marks, periods go inside the quotation marks.

THE QUEST OF QUESTION MARKS

Question marks (?) have a very specific purpose, but they have more uses than they may be given credit for. Here are some of the ways they are used.

Question marks are used to end a sentence that asks a question.

- Will you feed the dog for me?

Question marks also go at the end of a sentence that begins as a statement, but ends in a question.

- You will feed the dog, won't you?

GEEKOID

The punctus interrogativus was used beginning in the 8th century AD. It consisted of a period topped by a squiggle and cued an upward inflection in voice to signal a question. It is speculated that it was not used very much because questions were easily recognized by the syntax used. It went entirely out of use and the modern question mark was developed independently.

GEEK GLOSSARY

In 1962, the **interrobang** was introduced as "a twentieth century punctuation mark." Its purpose was to combine the question mark and an exclamation point to keep people from having to write "?!" to ask a question and show emotion.

Question marks can also be used to express doubt about something in a sentence, whether it is something specific like a date, or maybe validity of a fact you have just written.

- He said the concert will be Friday (?) after school.
- Jack's response to the promotion was a modest (?) smile.

GEEK AT A GLANCE

- Question marks go at the end of direct questions.

- Question marks also conclude sentences that begin as statements, but end in questions.

THE ENERGY OF EXCLAMATION POINTS

Exclamation points (!) are used to express strong emotion. They should be used sparingly.

Exclamations points often follow statements of only one or two words.

- Watch out!
- Well! Did you see that?

In formal writing, you would have very little use for exclamation points unless you are quoting something that contains one. In informal writing, you would use it to show something you find astonishing or surprising.

- He said the concert will be Friday (!) after school.
- He said the concert will be Friday after school!

GEEK*Speak:*

"Cut out all those exclamation marks. An exclamation mark is like laughing at your own jokes."
F. Scott Fitzgerald

GEEKOID

Do not use an exclamation point in the same sentence with other forms of punctuation, such as a period, comma, or question mark.

Use exclamation marks sparingly. To use several of them would be the same as writing in all capital letters. It would look like you're writing in a state of extreme excitement.

Do not use more than one exclamation point at the end of any sentence. One will be sufficient to express the emotion you intend to convey.

GEEKOID

The exclamation point is descended from a logotype for the Latin word io, meaning "joy," which was a capital "I" set over a lowercase "o." The design of the exclamation point was gradually streamlined to its present form.

GEEK AT A GLANCE

- Exclamation points follow interjections that express strong emotion.

- Use exclamation points sparingly.

THE CURE OF THE COMMON COMMA

The **comma (,)** has been said to have more uses than any other form of punctuation.

Maybe being so common is what what makes commas so troublesome, too, because it wins hands-down as being the most misapplied punctuation mark.

Comma placement can greatly affect the meaning of a sentence. Consider the difference in these two sentences.

- If you want to tell John, we won't stop you.

It means that John is going to be the recipient of information. Now look at this sentence.

The word **comma** comes from the Greek *komma*, which comes from *koptein*, meaning to cut off, as in cutting off one part of a sentence from another.

- If you want to tell, John, we won't stop you.

Quite the opposite of the first, this sentence makes John the one giving the information.

But comma use need not be confusing. Here are some things you need to know to correctly use this vital form of punctuation.

Use a comma to separate a series of three or more items, even before the **and** or any other connecting word. You do not need a comma to join only two items.

- John, Barbara, and Terrance planned the trip.
- John and Barbara planned the trip.

This rule applies even when the series of words are descriptive words that could each stand alone.

- Her hair was long, blonde, and curly.
- The campers returned tired, dirty, and happy.

 *In a series of three or more items, a comma goes before the conjunction.*

If you have two or more adjectives together whose meanings are dependent on each other, do not separate them by commas.

- Her mother wore a pale blue shirt.

Use a comma to separate two complete thoughts (clauses) joined by a conjunction.

- John bought a new car, and he took us for a ride.
- I wanted to go with him, but he had to leave early.

This sentence could easily be broken down into two separate sentences.

- John bought a new car.
- He took us for a ride.

If the sentence reads like this, you would not use the comma.

GEEK*Speak:*

"All morning I worked on the proof of one of my poems, and took out a comma; in the afternoon I put it back."
Oscar Wilde

- John bought a new car and took us for a ride.
  John bought a new car could stand alone, but **took us for a ride** couldn't.

GEEKOID

When you join two independent thoughts incorrectly with a comma, this is called a **comma splice**. Here is an example of this error.

John brought a new car, he took us for a ride.

There are a couple of ways to correct this: use a semi-colon instead of a comma, use a period and make two complete sentences, or add the conjunction as in the example.

John brought a new car; he took us for a ride.
John brought a new car. He took us for a ride.
John bought a new car, and he took us for a ride.

Use a comma following introductory words and phrases, such as these.

A **clause** is a group of words that has its own subject and verb. An **independent clause** is a clause that can stand on its own as a complete sentence. That's why it's called independent.

- At last
- Consequently
- Finally
- First
- However
- In addition
- Most likely

- Most likely, we will be the last to leave.
- First, let me thank all those who helped.
- Finally, the test results arrived.

Use a comma even when the phrases are longer.

- After she spoke her mind, she felt better.
- Since she is my cousin, she will be in the wedding.

GEEKOID

During the Renaissance, the printer Aldus Manutius set a standard by consistently using a period for a full stop and a slash to indicate a brief pause. Over time, this slash shortened and finally curled to become our modern comma.

Use a comma to set off non-essential phrases in a sentence. These phrases include information that is helpful, but not essential, to the sentence.

GEEK GLOSSARY

A **phrase** is a group of words that does not have its own subject and verb. It cannot stand alone.

- His new car, <u>a</u> <u>bright</u> <u>red</u> <u>Mustang</u>, rode like a dream.
- My mother, <u>who</u> <u>is</u> <u>taller</u> <u>than</u> <u>I</u>, stood nearby when I spoke.

When you are including information that is essential to the sentence, do not set that material off by commas.

- The boy who is the fastest will be chosen as captain.

All the information is needed to make the sentence be correctly understood, so none of it should be offset by commas.

Other forms of non-essential information would be interrupting elements, or words and phrases that break the flow of the sentence.

- I can come by Thursday or, <u>if</u> <u>you</u> <u>wish</u>, could wait until Friday.
- Sandra Young, <u>rather</u> <u>than</u> <u>Edward</u> <u>Townsend</u>, will be the meeting planner.

GUERRILLA GEEK

A **vocative** is a noun, pronoun, or noun phrase used in direct address. They may appear anywhere in a sentence.

Transitional words and independent comments may also be offset with commas, as in these sentences.

GEEKOID

Try this to help you decide if you need a comma or not: If the second clause does not begin with a subject of its own, do not use a comma.

- I was not notified, nevertheless, I will be at the meeting.
- We could not, on the other hand, forego the opportunity.
- It is not wise, in my opinion, to change our budget.

 Non-essential words in a sentence are set off by commas. Essential words are not.

Use a comma to set off the name of someone you are directly addressing.

- **John**, I asked you to open the door.
- He said, **Martha**, that we will not be able to go.

Use a comma to set off **appositives**, nouns or pronouns that rename or explain other nouns or pronouns.

GEEK*Speak:*

"Anyone who can improve a sentence of mine by the omission or placing of a comma is looked upon as my dearest friend."

George Moore

- John, **my brother**, will pick up the package.
- My dog, **the one with the brown patch**, came running.

Appositives may come before the noun or pronoun.

GEEKOID

When you have only the month and year of a date, you do not need a comma between them.

The following month, **July 1776**, proved to be historic.

- **The tall lady**, my mother, was the spokesperson.

Use a comma to set off contrasting elements of a sentence.

- The work was done by John, not Andrew.

Always use a comma to express dates.

- We celebrate our national independence on July 4, 1776.

When the date comes in the middle of text, a comma should always follow the year.

- July 4, 1776, is recognized as our country's birthday.

Commas are used to introduce a quotation.

- She said, "I don't intend to see him again."

Commas used with quotation marks should always go inside the quotation marks.

GEEKOID

When defining words are essential, do not set them off with a comma.

My brother John drove me to the airport.

In this sentence, John is essential to the sentence because the writer has several brothers.

• Our choir sang "The Hallelujah Chorus," but I did not sing along.

If you were to write "The Hallelujah Chorus" by itself, there would be no comma as part of the title, so you might wonder why the comma is included within the quotation marks, instead of coming after it. "Because standard American English says so" is the only answer available. Placing the comma within the quotation marks is correct, though it may not look it.

GEEKOID

Do not use a comma before a quote if the word **that** precedes the quote, or if the quote is otherwise woven into the sentence.

In her letter, she told me **that** "I don't intend to see him again."

 **GEEK AT A GLANCE**

- Commas are the most helpful, and yet most misused, form of punctuation.

- Commas help to separate items in a series.

- Commas separate descriptive words, but should be omitted if the modifiers are dependent on each other for meaning.

- Unnecessary phrases may be set off by commas. Essential words are not set off.

- Introductory words should be followed by a comma.

- Nouns of direct address should be set off with commas.

ALLOW ME TO INTRODUCE YOU

A **colon (:)** basically does one thing: it introduces.

The job of colons is to let you know something is coming. They can introduce a word, a phrase, a sentence, a quotation, or a list.

 *Colons can introduce a word, a phrase, a sentence, a quotation, or a list.*

Here are examples of each of these things a colon can do.

- John had one thing on his mind: food.
- Terry focused on one thing as well: making money.
- Mary's request was simple: to eat on time.
- Teresa had three favorite colors: green, blue, and red.

The word **punctuation** is derived from the Latin word "punctus," translated "point." Until the sixteenth century, the English word for punctuation was "pointing."

 *A **colon** lets you know something important is coming. It commands extra attention by causing you to pause instantaneously and prepare for what's ahead. A colon gives special emphasis to the thing(s) it introduces.*

Here are some other things a colon can do as well.

Colons are great for introducing lists. But a colon should never follow a verb or a preposition.

- Mr. Green's crops included: corn, peas, and okra. (Incorrect)
- Mr. Green had three main crops: corn, peas, and okra. (Correct)

Colons do follow introductory words like **as follows**, or **the following**.

> # GEEKOID
>
> When a colon is used within a sentence, the first word following the colon should begin with a lower case. When the colon introduces two or more sentences or a speech, dialogue, or an extract, the first word following the colon should be capitalized.

- Sarah's favorite colors were the following: red, pink, and yellow.

Colons are used in business letters and memos to follow the salutation. They are more formal than commas, which you would use in a friendly letter.

- Dear Mr. Jones:

Colons are often used to separate book titles from their subtitles.

- His new book was *Johnny on the Spot: A Guide to Efficiency.*

Colons are used in America to separate hours from minutes when writing about particular times.

- The party will be held at 7:30 p.m. in the fellowship hall.

In England, a period is often used instead of a colon, but a colon is customary here, and offers a more definite separation.

Colons separate chapters of the Bible from verse numbers.

- The text was taken from Proverbs 3:5-6.

GUERRILLA GEEK

A colon is not used after words like **namely** and **for example**. Here is correct punctuation for those words:

- Our main concerns were other factors, namely, time, money, and number of volunteers.

- Please pick a good student to help, for example, Judith.

Volume and page numbers are distinguished by colons when citing references.

- The article was found in *Dining Out* 3:5-8.

Colons also help to indicate ratios.

- The resolution passed 2:1.
- The ratio of vinegar to water was 3:1.

When used with quotation marks, the colon always goes outside.

- Please send me the following from the file marked "Confidential": the letter, the form, and the photos.
- This is the first line of Robert Frost's "The Road Not Taken": "Two roads diverged in a yellow wood."

Colons should never follow a verb or a preposition. Placing a colon after either of these would separate the verb or preposition from its respective object.

GEEK AT A GLANCE

- Colons introduce other words, and let you know something is coming.

- Colons have many functions. Here are some of their jobs:

  - introduce lists
  - follow salutations
  - separate book titles from subtitles
  - give Biblical chapters and verses
  - indicate volume and page numbers
  - show ratios

- When colons are used with quotation marks, colons go outside.

THE SUPER COMMA

The **semi-colon (;)** is used to separate items. It is more powerful than a comma, and indicates a more definite pause.

Semi-colons cannot end a sentence, but may be used to separate elements that are equal. When the separate-but-equal elements are related, you may join them with a semi-colon.

Here are some things a semi-colon can do.

Semi-colons can be a semi-period by offering almost a full stop between separate items of equal significance.

GEEKOID

A semi-colon is not a half colon—it can be considered to be a semi-period or a super comma.

- Bob is working on his graduate degree; Jane already has hers.
- Most workers favored the move; the evening crew did not.

Semi-colons are extremely helpful in organizing phrases that already have commas within them.

Semi-colons may be used as a super comma when they join elements that already contain commas within them. Too many commas could be confusing, but semi-colons can help separate the units into manageable bite sizes. See how confusing this sentence would be if we use only commas.

- Dates for interviews will be Tuesday, March 5, Wednesday, March 13, and Thursday, April 22.

See how much clearer this version is, this time with semi-colons.

- Dates for interviews will be Tuesday, March 5; Wednesday, March 13; and Thursday, April 22.

Semi-colons may be used to help separate a clause that begins with a conjunction or transition word.

- She wanted to go with us; however, she had a class in ten minutes.
- The student's paper was late; in addition, he did not follow proper format.

Elements separated by semi-colons must be of equal rank, but they do not have to be independent clauses (able to stand alone).

When used with quotation marks, semi-colons should be placed outside the quotation marks.

- He thought he had read the entire chapter on "Grammar and Style"; however, he was mistaken.

GEEK Speak:

"Words are only postage stamps delivering the object for you to unwrap."

George Bernard Shaw

GEEK AT A GLANCE

- Semi-colons are used to separate words of equal significance by offering almost a full stop between items.

- They may be used as a super comma between items that already contain commas within them.

- When semi-colons are used with quotation marks, the semi-colons are placed outside the quotation marks.

YOU MAY QUOTE ME

When you write, you may occasionally need to quote the words of other people. There are specific ways to indicate all kinds of quotations.

When writers include the words of other people in their writing, the words must be enclosed in quotation marks.

 *There are two kinds of quotation marks. **Double quotation marks** (" "), with which we're more familiar, and **single quotation marks** (' ').*

Both kinds of quotation marks come in sets, with each set having an opening quotation mark, and a closing one. The opening quotation mark points upward, and the closing mark points downward.

<u>Double</u> <u>quotation</u> <u>marks</u> have three primary functions: to indicate the use of someone's exact words; to set off words and phrases for special meanings; and to indicate titles of certain publications and artistic works.

GEEKOID

Following Johann Gutenberg's invention of the printing press in the 1400s, printers experimented with many signs and symbols to help their readers, but it wasn't until at least the late 1600s that standardized punctuation emerged.

Quotation marks are used to present the exact words of someone being quoted. Here is how they look when used like this.

- He simply said, "That idea will not work."
- When asked for his opinion, he said, "No comment."

Double quotation marks may also be used to set off unusual, slang, or coined phrases that your reader might not be familiar with.

Do not use quotation marks unless you are quoting the **exact** words of another person. If you are paraphrasing, no quotation marks are needed.

- The reporter was angry to see the editor "kill" her story.

This might also apply to words used in a tongue-in-cheek way.

- His "vacation" was of the honey-do variety.

Double quotation marks are used to enclose titles of short works such as journal articles, short stories, short poems, titles of songs, and chapter headings.

- His article "What Happens on Friday Night" appeared in last month's edition of *On the Town* magazine.

Names of shorter works are placed within quotation marks, while titles of longer pieces, or the works within which the shorter works are contained, are underlined or are set in italics.

GUERRILLA GEEK

If by chance you ever have a quote within a quote, within a quote, use double quotation marks, then single ones within those, and then go back to double ones within the single ones. But if you face this problem, your sentence needs to be reworded!

Single quotation marks are used to indicate a quote within a quote.

- Jill said, "She told me, 'I want to go along.' Those were her exact words."

<u>Block</u> <u>quotations</u> are used for very long quotation or excerpts of four lines or more. To indicate that you are quoting, set the text apart from the regular text by indenting your margins on each side by an extra five spaces and by leaving a blank line above and below the extract.

Ancient Greek writers had no system of punctuation to help them. All their letters ran together.

Note that no quotation marks are used around the material, but they should be used for any quoted material within the extract.

If the extract consists of more than one paragraph, leave a blank line between paragraphs.

Here is an example of how to treat a long quotation.

> John and Georgette saw quickly that they did not have all the facts. But they didn't know how to get them. It was at that time that the inspector offered them a letter that had been found at the scene.
>
> I know that none of you will understand my actions, but I assure you I am doing what is best for all involved. I will not be able to fully explain the situation to everyone's satisfaction, but trust me with what I am doing. I have taken into account factors that you will not know about, but you will see in the end that this is the wisest course.
>
> Stunned by the note, John and Georgette had no choice but to accept that they had no control over the situation. They silently returned the crumpled paper to the officer, and left with only their puzzled expressions revealing their thoughts.

GEEKOID

In the eighteenth century, Timothy Dexter wrote his book, *A Pickle for the Knowing Ones*, with no punctuation at all. In response to readers' demand for the book to be amended to include these helpful marks, he published a second edition, which included a page full of punctuation marks, noting that " ... I put in A nuf here and thay may peper and solt it as they please."

 **GEEK AT A GLANCE**

- Quotation marks should be used when you repeat words another person has said.

- Quotation marks come in two forms: double quotation marks for quotations, and single quotation marks for quotes within quotes. Each kind has an opening and a closing part.

- Long quotations of more than four lines in length should be presented in a block quotation, indented and single-spaced. No quotation marks are needed, but if quotations appear with the block quotation, use double quotation marks.

SOMETHING FOR CONTRACTIONS AND OTHER PAINS

Apostrophes (') may be small, but they have several jobs to do.

Described as an "elevated comma," the apostrophe is helpful in numerous ways.

Apostrophes are used to form possessives.

• <u>Mary's</u> dog was taken to the veterinarian.

> *Remember that apostrophes are not needed to show possession of personal and relative pronouns.*

ours	***not** our's*
yours	***not** your's*
hers	***not** her's*
whose	***not** who's (unless you mean who is)*
its	***not** it's (unless you mean it is)*

GEEKOID

The Apostrophe Protection Society was formed in 2001 by John Richards with the goal of preserving the correct use of the frequently misused punctuation mark. Others who wish to join the effort are urged to view and submit examples of incorrect use at www.apostrophe.fsnet.co.uk.

Apostrophes also show where letters have been omitted in contractions.

- He said, "I **can't** go hiking today."

Apostrophes may be used to indicate the omission of numbers, as well as letters.

- The Spirit of **'76** is still alive and well.
- The class of **'75** made its mark on the world.

Apostrophes can help indicate unusual pronunciation common to certain regions or dialects.

- It's **'bout** time you came to your senses!
- Hey, **y'all**.

Apostrophes are used to simply help clarify what you mean. Consider the term P's and Q's. These are plural words, not Possessive, but an apostrophe is used there to help separate the letters when you form their plurals. Without this useful form of punctuation, it would look like this: Ps and Qs.

GEEKOID

Before using a contraction, be sure you know what the contraction will mean. Some contractions can have several meanings. For instance, **What's** can mean **what is**, **what has**, **what does**, and **what was**.

GUERRILLA GEEK

You can also use an apostrophe to indicate the plural of symbols and numbers.

- List all the size **8's** in this column.
- Write the titles for all the **¶'s** when making an outline.

Some words are so commonly used in abbreviated forms, that they are now accepted without all of their letters. Because they are in such regular use, no apostrophe is needed.

- Who is on the **phone**? (instead of **telephone**)
- Have you ever been **possum** hunting? (instead of **opossum**)
- Go **Bama**! (instead of **Alabama**)

GEEK AT A GLANCE

- Apostrophes are best described as an elevated comma.

- Apostrophes have many uses:
  - show possession
  - help form contractions
  - indicate omission of letters
  - help form unusual pronunciations
  - form plurals of symbols and numbers

ENCLOSURES FOR EXPLAINING YOURSELF

Parentheses ( ) set off explanatory or qualifying remarks.

Parentheses let the reader know that the material enclosed is something extra.

• The storm hit at noon (right at lunch hour).

Right at lunch hour adds information that is helpful, but not essential, to the sentence. It is appropriately placed within parentheses.

 *Use parentheses for material that is important enough to be included, but not important enough to be a part of the main sentence.*

If you must add a comma with parenthetical material, add the comma after the closing parenthesis.

• The storm hit at noon (right at lunch hour), and caused a traffic jam.

GEEKOID

"The Phonetic Punctuation System" sketch was a piece in comedian Victor Borge's stage show based around the idea of verbalizing the punctuation marks in the English language.

Here are some of the ways parentheses can be used.

Parentheses may enclose numbers or letters that accompany items within a series.

- The plan called for (1) creativity, (2) teamwork, and (3) extra effort.

Parentheses may be used to clarify information provided in sentences. You'll find them used this way particularly in legal documents.

- The Party of the First Part (John Doe) and the Party of the Second Part (Agnes Brown) enter into this agreement.

This is an especially common way to specify monetary amounts.

- The asking price for the land was thirty thousand dollars ($30,000).

GUERRILLA GEEK

When you write, double check to be sure that every opening parenthesis has a closing one.

GEEKOID

Parentheses usually come in a set, with an opening parenthesis and a closing one, but a single parenthesis may be used in lists, such as an outline. Here is an example of how that would look.

1) Grammar
2) Nouns
3) What to capitalize
4) First words of sentences

GUERRILLA GEEK

When writing, people often include examples within parentheses. You may want to also consider using i.e. or e.g., which do not have parentheses.

i.e., Latin for id est, means "that is." It names something specific that has already been mentioned. It's used like this:

- The prince's older son will assume the throne, **i.e.**, William.

e.g., *exempli gratia*, means "for the sake of example." This sentence demonstrates the correct use of **e.g.**

- My favorite holidays are in the winter, **e.g.**, Thanksgiving and Christmas.

 *If you find that you are using too many parentheses to clarify or explain, check your writing. It is probably not clear. Parentheses should be the exception, not the rule.*

Parentheses also help to play down the importance of material you wish to de-emphasize.

- The offer of a smaller amount (only $500) was rejected.

GUERRILLA GEEK

Never use parentheses *within* parentheses. If you need something else within parentheses, use brackets. Also check your writing. If you need brackets and parentheses together, you probably need to edit and clarify your writing.

Putting the amount in parentheses this way almost helps you brush past it, without interruption to the sentence.

Parentheses can be helpful when referring to things outside the sentence.

A question within parentheses has its own punctuation, while the main sentence has its own.

- The views of the candidate have been expressed previously (see March 15, 2005 article.)

Parentheses may be used in a sentence to question or indicate uncertainty about material in the sentence.

- He had until June (or was it July?) to pay the fine.

GUERRILLA GEEK

When you have a see reference, like (see Penicillin), or a see also reference in parentheses, you do not capitalize the word see.

GEEK
AT A GLANCE

- Parentheses are used to set off additional, but not essential information.

- They are usually used in pairs, but there are some uses for single parenthesis.

- Do not overuse parentheses.

- Use brackets, not additional parentheses, if more explanation is needed within the parentheses.

JUST A COUPLE OF SQUARES

Brackets [ ] enclose comments, corrections, or additions within parenthetical material. They are not just square parentheses.

Brackets have limited, but particular, uses. In general, they are used to offer extra information within other parenthetical information.

You use brackets when you have a parenthetical remark within another parenthetical remark.

- These trees are found in warm climates (in Georgia and Alabama [especially on the Gulf Coast] and in Florida).

Brackets may indicate your own comments about a quotation you are using.

- The doctor said, "I am concerned [obviously he was worried] about the boy's condition."

Unlike parentheses, brackets never appear except in pairs.

An important use of brackets is to acknowledge an error. For example, if there is an error in a quotation, you are obliged to quote it exactly, but you would include the word [*sic*] immediately behind the incorrect information to let your reader know that you realize the error.

- Columbus sailed the ocean in 1495 [*sic*].

*Use [**sic**] to indicate that you are aware of a mistake, and that it is not your error.*

This is especially helpful when you use quotes that contain misspelled words, and you wish to let the reader know that the mistake is not yours.

• I am of Scottish decent [*sic*] and proud of it.

GEEK GLOSSARY

Sic is Latin for "thus, this way," and since it's a foreign word, it is always in italics. Since it is an entire word, and not an abbreviation, it has no period.

GEEK AT A GLANCE

• Brackets are used to present additional explanatory material within parenthetical material.

• An important use of brackets is with [*sic*], which is used to indicate the author's recognition of an error.

MISSING IN ACTION

Ellipsis points [...] indicate the omission of words. They consist of three periods in a row, with a space before and after each period.

Ellipsis points indicate that words have been omitted. There are several ways this handy device can be used.

Ellipsis points can be used anywhere in a sentence—in the beginning, middle, or end.

GUERRILLA GEEK

Although the proper term for this device is **ellipsis points**, it is commonly referred to as **an ellipsis**. The plural form is **ellipses**.

- They promised to love, honor ...
- We have witnessed a change in buying habits ... Customers are more price conscious.

Use ellipsis points when your intention is to "just trail off" in saying something so familiar that everyone already knows how it should be completed.

- "In the spring a young man's fancy..."

GEEK OID

Asterisks (* * *) are sometimes also used to indicate omission, but are now infrequently used this way.

When an ellipsis ends the sentence, add whatever punctuation you would normally add to the sentence, even if it is another period.

The **ellipsis** was first used in Old Norse in 200 BC, the first known existence of such verbal omissions in written language.

- "Can anyone explain why...?"

Use an ellipsis when an enumeration or list continues long beyond the items named.

- The student began to recite, "A, B, C... ."

An ellipsis may be used for emphasis. See how the following short groups of words are emphasized by being separated by ellipses.

- Do it soon... Do it today ... Do it now.

The word **ellipsis** comes from a Greek word meaning to fall short or leave out. It could indicate something omitted in the beginning, middle, or end of a sentence.

 **GEEK AT A GLANCE**

- Ellipsis points are commonly referred to as an ellipsis.

- This handy device indicates omission of words and may appear anywhere in a sentence.

- Ellipses are also used to "trail off" when it is unnecessary to continue with the thought because it is so well known.

- Ellipses may be used to emphasize items by adding space between them.

LET'S GET TOGETHER, YEAH, YEAH, YEAH

A **hyphen [-]** is most often used to join words together to make a compound word.

Hyphens have seemingly contradictory jobs. While they join words, they can also be used to separate words, or to indicate that a word continues on the next line when it must be divided.

Hyphens may be used to join two words that describe a word that follows.

The **hyphen** was introduced around the eleventh century to indicate that a word was continued on the next line.

• The award-winning show was held over four weeks.

Hyphens are particularly used to join adjective-noun compound modifiers.

• His company decided to begin working a four-day week.
• We were excited about the state-of-the-art equipment.

GUERRILLA GEEK

Compound descriptive words are hyphenated only when they precede the word they modify. If they follow the word, they are not hyphenated.

Hyphens may be used to accent the proper spelling or structure of a word.

- Do not confuse the words a-f-f-e-c-t and e-f-f-e-c-t.

Hyphens can help express particulars of speech, such as a stutter, or hesitation in speaking.

- "W-e-ll, let's see what we have here," was all he said.

Hyphens may help express regional or dialectic expressions.

- "He was just a-gaspin and a-shoutin' as he preached."

GUERRILLA GEEK

Sometimes you may have a "hanging hyphen," that is a hyphen that is not directly attached to another word. This happens when there are two hyphenated words that apply to the same base word.

- He was knowledgeable of nineteenth- and twentieth-century customs.

In this example, instead of repeating the word century, to which both nineteenth and twentieth apply, hyphenate them both, and leave the first one "hanging."

GEEK◯ID

You may divide a word over two lines, using a hyphen to connect the two parts, but do not divide a word over two pages.

Hyphens can be very useful when used within addresses and phone numbers.

- Our apartment was number 14-A.
- His cell number was 963-8840.

Hyphens should be used when numbers are written out as words.

GUERRILLA GEEK

Hyphens are called **en dashes** because they take up as much space as the letter **n** used to when type was actually set and each letter had a different width according to its shape.

- The twenty-three students lined up in formation for gym.

Hyphens may be used to indicate the omission of words for various reasons. The word <u>to</u>, in particular, is often implied by a hyphen.

- May – August are our busiest months.

GEEKOID

Do not use a hyphen when the words **from** and **between** are used. To use a hyphen with these would be redundant.

- The author lived between 1874-1945. (Incorrect)
- Between 1972 and 1975, I was a college student. (correct)
- I traveled abroad from September to November. (correct)

GEEK AT A GLANCE

- Hyphens are most often used to join words to make compounds, especially to join two words that together describe another word.

- Hyphens are used between numbers to join, and to separate them.

- Hyphens are also called en dashes because they were the width of the letter n when each letter was of unique width.

- Hyphens can be incorporated within words to indicate particular pronunciations.

ADDING JUST A DASH

The **dash [–]** is longer than the hyphen and has different functions.

Dashes are used mainly to create a definite break in the structure of a sentence.

- Come and see the teams—especially our Spartans—in the playoffs.

They can be used anywhere in the sentence, and do not necessarily have to be used in pairs.

- Peace—that was all he wanted.

GEEKOID

Dashes are called **em dashes** because they are the width an **m** would be back when type was set and letters had different widths according to their shapes.

GEEKOID

The invention of punctuation to mark the grammatical or logical structure of texts is generally attributed to Aristophanes of Byzantium. As chief librarian of Alexandria (c. 15 BCE) he was responsible for copying and annotating many works from classical Greek literature, adding breathings and accents as he went. His system was simple and divided text by dots placed at the end of words.

Dashes may help to indicate a break or shift in a sentence.

- I think—no, I am certain—that I gave her the message.

- Dashes are used within sentences to indicate a shift in structure

- Dashes are also called em dashes because they were the width of the letter m when type was set letter by letter and each letter had a different width.

THE VIRTUES OF THE VIRGULE

The **virgule (/)**, more commonly known as a **diagonal**, separates and divides elements from one another.

Virgules/diagonals/slashes may be used to indicate alternative word choices.

- He said we could all go eat and/or see a movie.
- The winner gets all the cola he/she can drink.

Slashes are used to indicate breaks in lines of poetry, as with this example from Robert Frost's famous poem, "The Road Not Taken."

- Two roads diverged in a yellow wood,/ And sorry I could not travel both/ And be one traveler, long I stood/ And looked down one as far as I could/ To where it bent in the undergrowth.

GEEK GLOSSARY

The proper name for a slash, though you don't hear this used often, is a **virgule**. It is also known as a **solidus**.

GEEK Speak:

"Ignorant people think it is the noise which fighting cats make that is so aggravating, but it ain't so; it is the sickening grammar that they use."

Mark Twain

Virgules are commonly used in citing dates.

* The statue was dedicated 1/24/78.
* The package was received on 10/15/04.

---

* The virgule is commonly known as a slash, or a diagonal. It is also called a solidus.

* It is used to indicate alternate word choices, and to indicate the end of a line of poetry.

* The most common use of the virgule is to separate the month, day, and year when the date is expressed in numerals.

IT'S ALL ABOUT STYLE

The first two sections of the book have discussed how to use words correctly when we write or speak, and how to use punctuation correctly when we write.

But even those two things are not enough. You need to know how to combine those elements effectively to make your writing express your thoughts precisely. Then, once you have your ideas on paper, you have to know how to polish your writing and make it perfect. That's where our hints on style come in handy.

HANDING DOWN GOOD SENTENCES

A **sentence** is a group of words that expresses a complete thought.

The elements required for a sentence are simple. There must be a subject and a predicate.

The subject of a sentence tells who does the action, and the predicate tells about what action is done.

Here are examples of complete sentences.

- The team won its **game**.
  (**Team** is the subject; **won its game** is the predicate.)

Sentences express thoughts in different ways, and are classified accordingly.

GEEKOID

Some people have a hard time understanding what a predicate is. Think of it this way: identify your subject, and consider everything else to be the predicate.

Declarative sentences tell what is or is not a fact.

- The ball is red.
- The cat did not come for its dinner.

<u>Interrogative</u> <u>sentences</u> convey information by asking questions.

- Is this your notebook?
- Which bus did you take?

<u>Imperative</u> <u>sentences</u> make commands or give instructions.

- Do your homework as soon as you get home.
- Lay the report on my desk when you are finished.

<u>Exclamatory</u> <u>sentences</u> express a thought as an exclamation, whether or not they are ended by an exclamation point.

- Oh, what a beautiful morning!
- Well, if that doesn't beat all.

GEEK GLOSSARY

Words that do not express a complete thought are called **fragments**.

GUERRILLA GEEK

A **pangram** is a sentence that contains all letters of the alphabet. By far the most well known is **The quick brown fox jumps over a lazy dog**.

Compound Sentences

When you join two simple sentences together, you make a <u>compound</u> <u>sentence</u>.

Compound sentences join two thoughts, either of which could stand alone, and make one long sentence.

- It started to rain. We ran for cover. (Simple)
- It started to rain, and we ran for cover. (Compound)

Complex Sentences

Complex sentences are made by joining a completed thought (that could stand alone—independent), with a clause that cannot stand alone (dependent).

- The food was prepared by two mothers. (Simple)
- The food, which arrived right on time, was prepared by two mothers. (Complex)

GEEKOID

Is this a complete imperative sentence? "Go!" Yes, because it has a subject (an implied subject—**you**), and a verb (go).

GUERRILLA GEEK

Would you believe there's even such a thing as a **compound complex** sentence? It's a combination of the two we just talked about.

- The students heard they might get out early, but since that didn't happen, they finished their classes.

GEEK AT A GLANCE

- A sentence is a group of words that expresses a complete thought.

- Every sentence must have a subject and a predicate.

- Words that do not form a complete sentence are called fragments.

- There are four types of sentences: declarative (make statements), interrogative (ask questions), imperative (give commands), and exclamatory (express exclamation).

- Compound sentences combine two complete (independent) thoughts.

- Complex sentences combine one complete thought (independent) with one incomplete (dependent) thought.

- Compound complex sentences are a combination of compound and complex sentences.

FRAGMENTS ARE ONLY PART OF THE STORY

Fragments are groups of words that do not form a complete sentence.

Here is an example to illustrate the difference between a fragment and a complete sentence.

• John ran. (**Complete**)

Although this sentence is short, it is complete. It has a subject, a predicate, and it expresses a complete thought. However, look at this one.

GEEK GLOSSARY

A **palindrome** is a word or sentence that reads the same forward as it does backward. Examples are **racecar**, **civic**, and the name **Hannah**. Entire sentences that read the same both ways are called **palingrams**. One of the most famous is **A man, a plan, a canal, Panama**. Another famous sentence that has even correct spaces properly positioned when read backwards, is **Able was I ere I saw Elba**, reportedly spoken by Napoleon, referring to his first sighting of Elba, the island where the British exiled him.

- Although he ran as quickly as he could. (**Fragment**)

This is not a complete sentence. It might be used to introduce a sentence, but it does not express a complete thought. It is a fragment.

Good, clear writing requires the use of complete sentences. Chronic use of fragments can make your writing seem, well, fragmented and haphazard.

But you know the old saying that even a stopped clock is right twice a day? The same could be said of fragments. Even with this imperfect sentence want-to-be, there are times when it is appropriate.

 *There are times when you can use fragments effectively, as long as you don't overdo them.*

Fragments may be used to make a point.

- Do we need to consider other plans? **Absolutely!** Are there times when our current system is not sufficient? **Without a doubt**.

The bold words are fragments, but they are used for effect to emphasize an answer. They are more appropriate here than long, complete sentences would be.

Fragments may be effective for writing lists. Readers would expect lists to be brief, so fragments would be appropriate here.

GEEKOID

Fragments can be used effectively as long as you only use them occasionally, and it is obvious that their use is intentional, not accidental.

The dorm meeting would cover these topics:

- Going home on the weekend.
- Cooking in your suite.
- Courtesy in the laundry room.

 *Fragments are certainly appropriate when you are writing a quote from someone who has spoken in fragments. In order to present the quote exactly as it was spoken, you must write it in fragments.*

- "Probably not," was the simple answer he gave.

 **GEEK AT A GLANCE**

- Fragments are groups of words that are not complete sentences.

- Even though fragments are incomplete, there are times when they may be used effectively.

CAPITAL OFFENSES

Some words should properly begin with capital letters. Here are some guidelines to help identify them.

There are some very general, and easy, rules that we'll review first of all.

The simplest rule is to begin every sentence with a capital letter.

• Today the sky is cloudless.

Begin quotations with a capital letter unless you indicate that you are starting in mid-quotation. This one's really a corollary of the rule about beginning sentences with a capital letter, because most quotations will be complete sentences.

GEEKOID

Do you capitalize the first word in a sentence following a colon? If the sentence that follows is brief, do not begin with a capital letter. If it is longer, and if it is one of several sentences that belong together, do begin with a capital letter.

• Margaret chose three vegetables for dinner: she preferred carrots, peas, and corn.
• Margaret chose three vegetables for dinner: She had always liked carrots, so she chose them, plus peas and corn for her meal. In addition, she had a helping of squash.

- James wrote in his journal, "Today was full of surprises."

After these very general rules, there are some very specific rules that go with capitalization.

Always capitalize proper nouns, which name particular things, not general ones. That includes the names of people and things. We would never begin anyone's name with a lower case letter.

- I gave the book to **jane**.

Written properly, this would be:

- I gave the book to **Jane**.

What word has a different meaning when it is capitalized? The word cited most often is "Polish." When it is capitalized, it means "relating to or coming from Poland"; when it is lowercased, it refers to the stuff one uses to polish cars and furniture.

 *Always capitalize proper nouns, especially names of people.*

Family names and titles, in particular, pose a problem. Do you capitalize those out of respect, or not?

Capitalize family titles when they precede a personal name, or are used instead of a name.

- I promised **Aunt Mary** I would help with dinner.
- Her mother, **Melinda**, was named after a close relative.

Professional titles, including civil and military titles, are capitalized only when they immediately precede a personal name, making it a part of the name. Titles that follow a name, or if they're used in place of it, are lowercased.

- Dean Paul John; Paul Johnson, **dean of the school**
- General George Ruby; the **general**

GEEKOID

Also, always capitalize the pronoun **I** and the exclamation **O**. But when you use **oh**, do not capitalize it unless it begins a sentence.
- **Oh**, how **I** hate Mondays.
- Be with us, **O** God, in our time of trial.

Capitalize words that "look divine," that is, those that refer to God, as well as pronouns that refer to Him.

- **God** parted the Red Sea, demonstrating **His** power.

Do not use a capital letter when referring to mythological gods, only when using specific mythological names.

- The Greeks worshipped many **gods**.
- The Greeks called **Zeus** the ruler of the heavens.

GUERRILLA GEEK

If a title follows a possessive word like my, his, your, or their, do not capitalize the word that comes after it.

- **My father** said he would be here soon.
- You and **your sister** look very much alike.

GEEKOID

Sometimes in very formal uses, you will see a title capitalized after a name.

You'll find this mostly in promotional or political contexts, or simply as a courtesy.

Capitalize certain words in book titles. Here are words to capitalize:

- The first word in the title: *The Elements of Style*
- Verbs and other important words: *How to Apply Make-up Correctly*
- Words that change the meaning in the title: *Courtship Through the Ages*

GUERRILLA GEEK

Some grammarians feel that there are some titles which should always be capitalized because of their importance, no matter if they appear with or without the name, such as high-level names of government officials. So don't be surprised if you see words like these below capitalized even when they do not precede a name.

- President of the United States
- Chief Justice of the Supreme Court

Do not capitalize

- **A**, **an**, or **the** unless they are the first word in the title: **A Day in the Life of a Mom**
- **Prepositions**, unless they are pivotal in the title: **Winning Through Perseverance**

Geographical directions should be capitalized in some cases. Maybe you haven't noticed (now you will), but sometimes directional words are capitalized and sometimes they aren't. Here's how you know when to do what.

Do not use all capital letters when writing e-mails. To do so is the equivalent of screaming at your recipient.

It all depends on whether you're just giving general directions, or referring to a portion of the country. The direction is not capitalized. The area of the country is. In other words,

- Go **south** to reach the **South**.

This includes words like central, west, etc.

- The **central** portion of the town was undeveloped.
- We moved **west** to avoid the storm.
        But
- We heard that **Central Park** is a major attraction in New York City.
- The old **West** has many stories to tell.

Countries and city names should be capitalized.

- <u>France</u>

Also capitalize the names that include country names: <u>French fries</u>, <u>Belgian</u> <u>waffles</u>. Some style books differ on this, but no matter which way you prefer, be consistent.

When the word **Greater** is included as part of the city name, capitalize it as well: **Greater Chicago**.

- <u>Atlanta, Georgia</u>
- We went to the <u>Smokey Mountains</u> on vacation.

GEEKOID

Note in this example about the **Smokey Mountains** that **the** is not capitalized. Use lowercase unless you are sure it is a part of the proper name. Most of the time it won't be.

But when the proper name is not used, do not capitalize it.

- We went to the <u>mountains</u> on vacation.

Use lowercase when writing about seasons, except in poetry, where the seasons are often personified (given human characteristics).

- Soon it will be **summer**.
- Here comes **Spring**, tip-toeing in.

Always capitalize names of days of the week, months, and holidays.

- The library will be closed on **Monday**, **July** 4, in celebration of **Independence Day**.

GUERRILLA GEEK

School subjects should be capitalized only when they refer to languages: history, **English**, **French**, math. But do capitalize proper course names: **Math for Mechanics**, **Physics at a Glance**, and **Easy English**.

GEEKOID

Names of decades are either spelled out in lowercase letters, or expressed in numerals.

- The sixties were a pivotal time in history.
- The 1970s saw our country at war.
- The twenty-first century was marked by concern for our computers.

GUERRILLA GEEK

Note that no apostrophe is needed when referring to decades, even when they are expressed in numerals.

GEEK AT A GLANCE

- Some words should begin with a capital letter.

- The first word in a sentence is always capitalized.

- Proper nouns, especially names of people, should always begin with a capital letter.

- Words in book titles should be capitalized; prepositions within the title, and articles (a, an, and the) should not be unless they are pivotal to the meaning.

- Professional and other titles should be capitalized when they immediately precede a name, but are usually not capitalized when they follow the name or are used alone.

- Names of days of the week, months, and holidays should be capitalized.

- Eras and decades should not be capitalized when spelled out.

PUTTING MODIFIERS IN THEIR PLACE

When descriptive words are misplaced in a sentence, it can be comical at best and confusing at worst. Either way, it is always misleading.

We already know from an earlier chapter what modifiers are. They're words that help describe other words. It is important that these descriptive words be placed correctly in relation to each other.

 *Even a single misplaced word can entirely change the meaning of a sentence.*

Misplaced Modifiers

Sometimes we have all the information we need in a sentence, yet it reads poorly because the words are not in correct order. Think about what this sentence says:

- Tony returned the coffeepot to the store that was defective.

Do you think the store was defective? No. It's the coffeepot, and yet the words **that was defective** are nearer to the word **store**, so that looks like the word being modified.

GEEKOID

It is estimated that more than 750 million people use the English language. Only about 350 million use it as their primary language.

A better sentence would be:

- Tony returned the **coffeepot that was defective** to the store.

An even better one would be:

- Tony returned the **defective coffeepot** to the store.

Now the meaning is accurate. The coffeepot didn't work, so he returned it.

Dangling Modifiers

This very descriptive term probably brings to mind an image of words twisting in the wind, longing for a solid place to actually attach themselves. That's exactly what they are: words that do not properly modify what is intended in the sentence.

Dangling modifiers are words or phrases that do not properly modify the part of the sentence the writer intends them to.

- Unable to remember his words,
  we watched as the singer struggled with his performance.

Who is unable to remember words in this sentence? Is it **we**? No, it is the singer.

The sentence could correctly be rewritten a couple of different ways:

- **Unable to remember his words**, the **singer** struggled with his performance.

OR

- We watched as the <u>**singer**</u>, <u>**unable to remember his words**</u>, struggled with his performance.

GUERRILLA GEEK

Squinting modifiers are modifiers whose intended object is unclear. These may also be called **two-way modifiers** because there are usually a couple of words they could logically modify.

- People who overeat frequently experience health problems.

Which word does frequently modify? Overeat? Experience? It's hard to tell. There are a couple of ways you could interpret this sentence.

- **People who overeat frequently** could be the subject.

OR

It could mean that if people eat too much, they **frequently experience health problems**.

Be sure your sentences are worded carefully so that their meanings are clear.

Here's an example of a modifier trying to describe something not even in the sentence.

- Having missed a day of school, a doctor's excuse was required.

Who missed a day of school? The sentence doesn't say. We are not told who missed the day of school. But we know that a noun or pronoun is needed to fix this sentence.

GUERRILLA GEEK

Anytime you have introductory words to a sentence followed by a comma, check to see that the first words after the comma relate to the introductory words.

- **Having missed a day of school**, I was required to bring a doctor's excuse.
- **Having missed a day of school**, he was required to bring a doctor's excuse.

Limiting Modifiers

The examples above show how a phrase, improperly placed, can change the entire meaning of your sentences.

Sometimes, it takes one word being out of place, to result in a sentence that doesn't mean at all what you intended. That's the case with **limiting modifiers**, single-word modifiers that have the power to change your meaning entirely. Examples include **almost**, **even**, **exactly**, **hardly**, **just**, **nearly**, **only**, and **scarcely**, just to name a few.

Take a look at how placement of limiting modifiers can change the meaning of other words.

- The teacher knew the boy.
- <u>Even</u> the teacher knew the boy.
  (This means that everyone, even the teacher, knew the boy. The emphasis here is on the boy.)
- The teacher knew <u>even</u> the boy.
  (The emphasis here is on the teacher and the fact that she knew everyone, including the boy.)

Here's another one:

- Mary had time for me.
- <u>Only</u> Mary had time for me.
  (This means that the only person who had time for me was Mary. The emphasis is on Mary.)
- Mary <u>only</u> had time for me.
  (This means that Mary only had time for one thing, and it was me.)
- She had <u>only</u> time for me. (She had nothing but time to offer.)
- She had time for <u>only</u> me.
  (Mary had no time for anyone except me.)

GEEK*Speak:*

"English usage is sometimes more than mere taste, judgment, and education—sometimes it's sheer luck, like getting across the street."

E.B. White

GEEK
AT A GLANCE

- Descriptive words in a sentence must be placed properly to portray a writer's intended meaning.

- Misplaced modifying (describing) words in a sentence can change the meaning of your sentence.

- Dangling modifiers, words that do not seem to be attached to an object, often introduce a sentence, followed by a comma. Always make sure that the first word after the comma is the correct object for the introductory words.

- Even though limiting modifiers are only one word, they still have the power to change the entire meaning of a sentence when not properly placed.

HEARING VOICES

Verbs used in our everyday sentences come in two voices: active and passive.

A verb is in **active voice** when the subject in the sentence performs the action.

- Alexis recorded the program while we were gone. (Alexis, the subject, does the action.)
- We recorded the program when we returned. (We, the subject, does the action.)

 Although most writing should be in active voice, there is a time and place for passive as well.

A verb is in **passive voice** when the action is performed upon the subject.

- The program was recorded by Alexis while we were gone. (The action is performed upon the recording.)
- The recording was watched by everyone when we returned. (The action is performed, again, on the recording.)

GEEK*Speak:*

"English is a funny language; that explains why we park our car on the driveway and drive our car on the parkway."

Anonymous

You will want most of your writing to be in active voice. It is more direct, and it has more energy. Use of active voice usually results in clear sentences. The passive voice is more indirect, and therefore, might be considered weaker. You might choose one voice over the other, depending on the effect you desire.

There are definitely times when passive voice is appropriate, for instance, when you want to be less confrontational. Consider this example:

- John left the copier on overnight. (Active—it might sound accusatory.)
- The copier was left on overnight. (Passive)

In a case like this, the passive voice would avoid fixing blame on anyone, but would accurately express the problem. You might use it when you don't know who is to blame.

 **Passive voice** *is also used when you just want to emphasize the facts, not the people doing them.*

- The proposal to reroute the road was met with stiff opposition.

In this example, you don't have to point out who opposed the proposal. The important thing is that it was opposed.

GEEK*Speak:*

"What is required is not a lot of words, but effectual ones."
Seneca

- Verbs in sentences are in active or passive voice.

- Active voice means that the subject does the action.

- Passive voice means that the subject was acted upon.

- Although most writing should be in active voice, there are times when passive voice is useful. It can help you avoid blaming someone for an action, or can state the action when you don't know who is to blame. In any case, it can emphasize the action instead of the person doing it.

WHERE GEOMETRY AND GRAMMAR COLLIDE

Parallel structure means expressing items in a sentence in similar ways so that they are consistent with each other. This will produce balance in your sentences.

Here are some particular ways you can help your writing flow by being aware of parallel structure.

With Gerunds

Gerunds are simple verbs that have had **ing** added to them. After that, they become nouns. When you use these words in a series, make sure all the words are in the same gerund form. Take a look at this example.

- Ashley likes **reading**, **sewing**, and **to cook**.

Not all of the items are expressed in the same way, so there is no parallel structure here. Look at this corrected sentence.

- Ashley likes **reading**, **sewing**, and **cooking**.

If you see this sentence, it looks and reads better; if you hear it spoken, it certainly sounds smoother, with all the words in the series being more uniform.

With Infinitives

Infinitives are verbs that are preceded by the word "to." When you choose to use that form with several items, be sure to make them all the same.

- Ashley likes <u>to read</u>, <u>to do sewing</u>, and <u>cooking</u>.

Let's edit the sentence so that the infinitive forms are all alike.

- Ashley likes <u>to read</u>, <u>to sew</u>, and <u>to cook</u>.

Now there is parallel structure.

With Adverbs

Be careful also when you use <u>ly</u> words.

- The employees worked <u>quietly</u>, <u>quickly</u>, and <u>in an efficient manner</u>.

The correct way to express these words in a parallel way would be like this:

- The employees worked <u>quietly</u>, <u>quickly</u>, and <u>efficiently</u>.

GEEK Speak:

"Prefer the short word to the long; the concrete to the abstract; and the familiar to the unfamiliar. But: Modify these guidelines in the light of the occasion, the full situation, which includes the likely audience for your words."

Jacques Barzun

Try reading what you've written aloud to see if all items sound as though they have been expressed in a parallel way.

With Lists

Whether you are using a numbered list, or you just have a list of items following a colon, make sure that all items are kept in the same form.

- His job was threefold: <u>to interview prospective students</u>, <u>to visit with them at their schools</u>, and <u>asking them to come for College Day</u>.

Correctly written, this sentence should be expressed in either of these ways:

- His job was threefold: <u>to interview prospective students</u>, <u>to visit with</u> <u>them at their schools</u>, and <u>to ask them to come for College Day</u>.
- His job was threefold: <u>interviewing prospective students</u>, <u>visiting with</u> <u>them at their schools</u>, and <u>asking them to come for College Day</u>.

GEEK OID

To help make sure your thoughts are expressed in a parallel way, when you proofread, be sure to double-check when you come across the words **and** and **or**. Those may connect items that you need to check for faulty parallelism.

- When you write, similar items should be expressed in similar ways. This is called parallel structure.

- Not only in lists, but with any series, all items should be expressed in the same way.

TRIMMING THE FAT

Good writing is free of excess words, which can make it bulky and difficult to read. Trimming the fat is one way to make it clearer and more effective.

There are several targets in writing when you think about cutting away excess.

Shorter Words

Let's start trimming the most basic unit in a sentence, the words. Why use a longer word when a shorter one will do? Shorter ones are easier to understand and are more direct than their longer counterparts.

Here are some words we commonly use, especially in formal writing, and suggestions for shorter substitutes.

Longer word	Shorter substitute
anticipate	expect
cooperate	help
facilitate	help
forward	send
inasmuch	since
indicate	show, reveal
personnel	people

prior to	before
presently	now
submit	give
terminate	end
utilization	use

Wordy Phrases

As you are making efficient word choices, you will also want to choose words that may be used in the place of bulky phrases. Here are some leaner choices for those times.

GEEKOID

In your zeal to use shorter words, don't be tempted to use unorthodox spellings because they might be shorter. Don't use "thru" for "through," or "scuse" for "excuse." Traditional spelling is always the standard.

Phrases	Substitutes
A considerable number of	many
A number of	some, several
A small number of	a few
A sufficient amount of	enough
Adverse impact on	hurt
Afford the opportunity	allow
Along the lines of	like
Are of the same opinion	agree
Arrive at the conclusion	conclude

GEEK Speak:

"When I see a paragraph shrinking under my eyes like a strip of bacon, I know I'm on the right track."

Peter DeVries

As a consequence	because
Ascertain the location of	find
At such time as	when
At the present time	currently, now
Based on the fact that	since, because
Be aware of the fact that	know

GEEK*Speak:*

"Avoid the elaborate, the pretentious, the coy, and the cute. Do not be tempted by a twenty-dollar word when there is a ten-center handy, ready and able."

E.B. White

Being of the opinion that	I believe
Came to a realization of	realized
Cannot be avoided	must, should
Come to a conclusion	conclude
Concerning the subject of	about
Considering that	because, since
Despite the fact that	although
Draw your attention to	point out, show

GEEKOID

It is important to use words in your writing that people are accustomed to hearing. For example, words like "heretofore" are reserved for very formal writing. For most other purposes, use "before now" or "previously."

Due to the fact that	since
Each and every one	each
Excessive number of	too many
Extend an invitation	invite
For the purpose of	to, for
Give an indication of	show
Give consideration to	consider
Has a tendency to	often
Has the ability to	can
Has been proven to be	is
In a position to	can, may, will
In a timely manner	promptly, on time
In addition to	besides, also
In all likelihood	probably
In close proximity to	near
In large measure	largely
In spite of the fact that	although
In the event that	if
In the final analysis	finally
In the majority of cases	usually
In the midst of	during, amid
In the near future	soon
In view of the fact that	since
Is aware of the fact	knows
It is imperative that we	we must

GEEKSpeak:

"Abide by the general rule: the fewer words the better."
Jacques Barzun

It is my understanding	I understand
It is often the case that	often
Last but not least	finally
Make a decision	decide
Make a purchase	buy
Make an examination of	examine
None at all	none
On a daily (or regular) basis	daily, regularly
On the grounds that	because
Owing to the fact that	since, because
Place an emphasis on	stress
Present time	present, now
Provided that	if
Reach a conclusion	conclude, decide
Subsequent to	after
That being the case	therefore
To a certain degree	somewhat
Until such time as	until
Utilize or utilization	use
With regard to	concerning, about

Now that you've started to streamline your writing, you'll find that there are other places you can cut fat, too.

Unnecessary opening words—One of the best ways to trim down writing is to eliminate unnecessary words at the beginning of your sentences.

- **There** were boys in the hallway that stood in our way.
- **It** was easy for us to decide the winner.

This sentence could be more concisely expressed this way:

- Boys in the hallway stood in our way.
- We could easily decide the winner.

<u>Double Verbing</u>—One of the quickest ways to bog down your writing is to add too many verbs. Cut out the extra verbs and your writing will immediately improve. Look at these examples to see how cutting out extra action words can lighten your writing.

- Today I **am writing** to **try** to **tell** you about the advances we **have made** on this project.

See how much clearer this version is without the extra verbs.

- Today I **will tell** you about the advances on our project.
        Or better yet,
- Here **are** the advances on our project.

GEEK*Speak:*

"I only want to use words that real people say."

W.B. Yeats

<u>Too many prepositions</u>—There's nothing like an appropriate preposition to tie words together, but it's possible to use too many of them at one time. Look at this over-use and how easy it is to correct it.

- The bank **around** the corner **in** the park **by** the restaurant is closed today.

There are three prepositional phrases in this sentence. It is no wonder that it is bulky and awkward to read. Try minimizing that number, or doing away with them altogether to make this sentence more readable.

- The bank **around** the corner is closed today.
    OR
- The local bank is closed today.

It's not only *too many* prepositions that can add unwanted bulk to your writing, but also unnecessary ones. Here are some examples where prepositions could be cut, and the deletion would result in better writing. Words that could easily be deleted are in bold.

- Where did that ball go **to**?
- She could not help **from** laughing at the incident.
- Tabby fell off **of** the chair as she played with the string.
- The waiting is now over **with**.
- I'm not **for** sure we'll be able to make the deadline.

- Good writing is free of extra and unnecessary words.

- Choose simple words instead of longer, more formal ones.

- Choose shorter phrases, or even single words, instead of longer, cliché phrases when possible.

CHOOSING YOUR WORDS WISELY

Be selective in choosing just the right words when you write. Be sure to get the ones with the meanings you need, and not a word that looks or sounds similar.

There are many words that may sound like other similar ones, but whose meanings are completely different. It is important to know and use these correctly in order to set yourself apart from others who don't know the finer points.

Here are some words you should know to be a real grammar geek!

Accept – to receive
Except – to leave out

Access – a way to get inside
Assess – to evaluate
Excess – too much

Adapt – to adjust to something
Adopt – to make something your own

Addition – something added
Edition – a particular published book

Adverse – opposing
Averse to – reluctant

GEEK GLOSSARY

A **malapropism** is the use of an incorrect word in place of a similarly sounding correct one.

Advice – opinion as to what should be done
Advise – to offer advice to

GEEK*Speak:*

"I do here, in the Name of all the Learned and polite Persons of the Nation, complain ... that our Language is extremely imperfect; that its daily Improvements are by no means in proportion to its daily Corruptions, that the Pretenders to polish and refine it have chiefly multiplied Abuses and Absurdities..."

Jonathan Swift, *Proposal for Correcting*, 1712

Affect – to influence
Effect – the result of something

A lot – many
Alot – incorrect; do not use this

All ready – prepared
Already – by this time

Allude – to draw attention in a general manner
Elude – to defy or baffle
Refer – to mention specifically

Altar – where one worships
Alter – to change

Altogether – entirely
All together – everyone or everything in one place

Among – comparison of more than two things
Between – comparison of two items

Anecdote – a short story that illustrates a point
Antidote – a cure

Apiary – where bees are kept
Aviary – where birds are kept

Assure – to set one's mind at rest
Ensure – to make sure from harm
Insure – usually means to guarantee life or property against risk

Bazaar – a marketplace
Bizarre – weird

GEEK *Speak:*

"Notice the decisions that other writers make in their choice of words and be finicky about the ones you select from the vast supply."
William Zinsser

Born – beginning life
Borne – carried, endured

Breach – a fracture or rift
Breech – the back of something

Bus – a large motor vehicle
Buss – a kiss

Callous – uncaring
Callus – a hardened bump on your skin

Can – having the ability
May – having permission

Capital – seat of government
Capitol – the actual building that
houses the government

Carat – the weight of precious stones
Caret – a mark of punctuation
Carrot – an orange spindle-shaped
edible root

Censor – to remove offensive elements
Censure – to criticize or blame

Cite – to quote or document
Sight – vision
Site – a place

Coarse – rough
Course – a passage or route

Complement – something that completes
Compliment – noun: praise; verb: to praise

Confidant – one to whom secrets are entrusted
Confident – self-assured

Council – a group that advises
Counsel – to advise

GEEK GLOSSARY

An **oxymoron** is the juxtaposition of seemingly contradictory terms. Examples would be **jumbo shrimp** and **bittersweet**.

GEEK*Speak:*

"Use the right word,
not its second cousin."
Mark Twain

Dear – loved
Deer – an animal

Desert – a dry, arid place
Dessert – sweet food at the end of a meal

Device – an object
Devise – to create or invent

Die – to stop living
Dye – to change the color of something

Disinterested – impartial
Uninterested – not interested

Dual – two
Duel – a fight

Elicit – to coax out
Illicit – illegal

Eminent – distinguished
Imminent – about to happen

Envelop – to wrap something
Envelope – paper that holds a letter

Exalt – to praise
Exult – to rejoice

GEEK Speak:

"The English language is rich in strong and supple words. Take the time to root around and find the ones you want."
William Zinsser

Exceed – to surpass
Accede – surrender

Famous – widely known
Infamous – having a notorious reputation

GEEK*Speak:*

"Whatever one wishes to say, there is one noun only by which to express it, one verb only to give it life, one adjective only which will describe it. One must search until one has discovered them, this noun, this verb, this adjective, and never rest content with approximations, never resort to trickery, however happy, or to vulgarisms, in order to dodge the difficulty."

Flaubert

Fare – a price
Fair – impartial

Farther – references to physical distance
Further – reference to a figurative distance

Faze – to disturb
Phase – a period of time (noun)
    – to do gradually (verb)

Fewer – refers to individual, countable items
Less – refers to general amounts

Flaunt – to show off
Flout – to openly defy

Forbear – to resist
Forebears – ancestors

Formally – dressed up; proper
Formerly – at a previous time

Forth – onward
Fourth – after third

Gaff – a spear (noun); to spear (verb)
Gaffe – a blunder

Eighty percent of the information stored in the world's computers is in English.

The longest English word to appear in standard English dictionaries is: pneumonoultramicroscopicsilicovolcanoconiosis (45 letters). This is the name of a lung disease suffered by miners. It first appeared in *Webster's New International Dictionary* and then later in the second edition of the *Oxford English Dictionary*.

There are quite a few other very long words in some specialties, such as science, but these words do not appear in standard dictionaries. The longest of these is the term for the formula $C_{1289}H_{2051}N_{343}O_{375}S_8$, which has 1,913 letters.

Genius – high level of ability
Genus – classification of a species

Hear – to listen
Here – at this place

Hoard – to stash
Horde – a crowd

Human – related to mankind
Humane – compassionate

Immoral – not moral
Immortal – never dying

Impair – to limit
Impede – to stand in the way of

GEEKOID

A recent sketch during an airing of *The Man Show* demonstrated the importance of knowing the difference between similar words. The hosts set up a booth with a large banner asking support to "End the Suffrage of Women." **Suffrage**, of course, means the right to vote. But women mistakenly thought it meant **suffering**. Numerous women enthusiastically signed the petition, saying it was about time, never realizing that they were working to end their own right to vote!

Imply – to hint at something
Infer – to draw a conclusion

Incredible – defying belief
Incredulous – skepticism or doubt

Intelligent – being smart
Intelligible – understandable

Its – shows ownership
It's – a contraction meaning it is

People often use the word **irregardless** when they actually mean **regardless**. **Irregardless** is not a word and should never be used. The less part of **regardless** already means **without**.

Lend – using temporarily
Loan – something that is used temporarily

Lesson – instruction
Lessen – to reduce

Liable – likely to
Libel – defamation of character in writing or by pictures/signs

Marital – relating to marriage
Martial – relating to military matters

Moral – right conduct
Morale – state of mind

GUERRILLA GEEK

Want to learn an interesting new word? It's not likely to be confused with anything else, but you'll be super geek chic for knowing it. The word is **octothorpe**, but you probably call it a pound sign. It looks like this: #. There's a story about how this symbol got its name. Back when computers were just beginning to be a big deal, Bell Labs engineer Don Macpherson went to instruct the Mayo Clinic in the use of a new telephone system. One of the doctors asked for the official name of the pound sign, and Macpherson, on the spot, said the first thing that came to mind: **octothorpe**. Here's where the word came from: octo for eight points of the symbol; **thorpe** because Macpherson was at that time active in a group to try to get Jim Thorpe's Olympic medals returned from Sweden. That part of the word was a tribute to Thorpe. Bell employees "in" on the joke starting using the new word in inter-office memos, but apparently it leaked out, because it started showing up in incoming correspondence as well.

Nauseated – an uneasy feeling in your stomach
Nauseous – the thing that makes your stomach uneasy

Parameter – established limit
Perimeter – border around something

Pare – to trim
Pair – two of a kind
Pear – a fruit

Peak – the highest point
Peek – to see
Pique – to intrigue

Perpetrate – to carry out
Perpetuate – to make last

Precede – to come before
Proceed – to go forward

Precedence – priority
Precedents – established rules

Preview – to see in advance
Purview – scope, or limits of

Principal – the most important
Principle – a fundamental truth

GEEK*Speak:*

"The words you choose to say something are just as important as the decision to speak."
Anonymous

GEEK GLOSSARY

Homographs and **homograms**, which are synonyms, refer to words that are spelled the same but differ in meaning, derivation, or pronunciation.

Prophesy – to predict
Prophecy – prediction

Prostate – a male gland
Prostrate – stretched out on the ground

Quiet – silent
Quite – to a certain extent

Rack – a display stand
Wrack – ruin or destruction

Respectfully – in an honorable way
Respectively – coordinated in order of things mentioned

Sea – body of water
See – to view

Sit – to be at rest
Set – to place

Soar – to fly over
Sore – painful

Stationary – standing still
Stationery – writing paper

Taught – instructed
Taut – tense, without slack

GEEKOID

Of all the words in the English language, the word **set** has the most definitions.

GUERRILLA GEEK

Here's a trick to help you remember the correct word you need for writing paper. The correct word is **stationery** (which ends in **ery**, but it's very similar to **stationary** (this word ends in **ary**). Think about the envelope that the paper will go with—envelope starts with an **e**, so use the word with an **e** in it!

Their – possessive form of they
There – indicates location
They're – contraction for "they are"

Through – into or out of; finished
Threw – past tense of throw
Thorough – careful or complete
Thru – slang form of through
Though – nevertheless

To – toward
Too – also
Two – more than one, less than three

Typical – conforming to the norm
Atypical – unusual, irregular

Vary – to change
Very – much

Veracious – truthful
Voracious – greedy

Waive – to give up a right or
privilege
Wave – to motion with the hands

Waver – to change
Waiver – to suspend, or make an
exception

Weak – not strong
Week – seven days

Whose – possessive pronoun
Who's – "who is" or "who has"

Your – possessive pronoun
You're – "You are"
Yore – past times

GEEK*Speak:*

"The greater part of
the world's troubles
are due to questions of
grammar."
Michel de Montaigne

RIDDING YOURSELF OF REDUNDANCIES

A great way to trim your sentences is to eliminate redundancies, or words that mean the same thing. Why use two words when you can use one just as effectively?

Here are some words people commonly use together. Stop and think about each one as you read the list and see how they repeat themselves.

absolutely certain
adequate enough
advance planning
a.m. in the morning
and also
and etc.
as an added bonus
ascend upward
ask the question
assemble together
ATM machine
autobiography of my life
basic essentials
basic fundamentals
biography of his life
blend together
cash money
close proximity

closed fist
combine together
completely finish
completely full
completely unanimous
connect together
consensus of opinion
continue on
continue to persist
cooperate together
deadly killer
each and every
each individual
endorse on the back
end result
exact replica
exactly the same
excised out
factual information
fewer in number
final conclusion
foreign imports
free gift
future planning
future predictions
HIV virus
honest truth
identical match
initial prototype
joint cooperation
large in size

GEEKOID

When you use **et cetera**, which means **and other things**, do not make the mistake of putting **and** before it. To do so would be redundant.

major breakthrough
may possibly
merge together
mix together
most optimum
mutual cooperation
necessary requirement
new innovation
old adage
old antique
ongoing evolution
outside periphery
overused cliché
past history
past memory
PIN number
please RSVP
p.m. at night
possibly may
protest against
protrude out
rarely ever
real fact
recur again
refer back
resemble in appearance
return back
rough estimate
safe haven
same identical
strangle to death

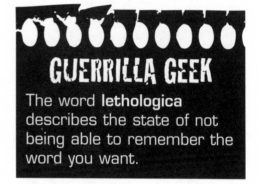

GUERRILLA GEEK

The word **lethologica** describes the state of not being able to remember the word you want.

sum total
surround on all sides
sworn affidavit
temporary reprieve
the reason is because
total entirely
totally monopolize
true facts
two twins
unexpected surprise
usual rule
valuable asset
very unique
viable alternative
VIN number
whole entire
widow of the late
widower of the late

GEEK*Speak:*

"For me, words are a form of action, capable of influencing change."
Ingrid Bengis

GEEK AT A GLANCE

- Redundant word use can make writing bulky and difficult to read.

- Be aware of redundancies in your writing and eliminate unnecessary words.

AIN'T NOTHING LIKE THE REAL THING

Close only counts in horseshoes! Words that are almost correct, but not quite, can make even good writing look careless.

Check your work carefully to be sure you have spelled every word correctly. Spell check should catch most misspellings, but it won't catch legitimate words used out of context. You should read your work carefully to be sure that none slip by and make your work look less credible.

Here are some words that are commonly misspelled.

acceptable
accidentally
accommodate
acquire
acquit
a lot
amateur
anoint
apparent
argument
atheist
balloon
believe
bellwether
business
calendar

GEEKOID

Noam Chomsky estimated that there are about 500,000 descriptive rules for any language that a speaker has to know about word order (syntax), pronunciation, word formation, and sentence structure before he can be a fluent speaker of a language.

camouflage
category
cemetery
changeable
collectible
column
commemorate
committed
conscience
conscientious
conscious
consensus
corps
daiquiri
definite(ly)
dilemma
discipline
disappoint
dormitory
drunkenness
dumbbell
ecstasy
embarrass(ment)
equipment
exhilarate
exceed
existence
experience
February
fiery
foreign

GEEK Speak:

"Correct spelling, indeed, is one of the arts that are far more esteemed by schoolma'ams than by practical men, neck-deep in the heat and agony of the world."
Henry Louis Mencken

gauge
genealogy
government
grammar
grateful
guarantee
harass
height
hierarchy
humorous
ignorance
immediate
independent
indispensable
inoculate
intelligence
jewelry
judgment
kernel
leisure
liaison
library
license
lightning
maintenance
maneuver
medicine
medieval
memento
millennium
miniature

GEEKSpeak:

"May the words be
very clean and sharp
like good knives."
John Steinbeck

minuscule
mischievous
misspell
neighbor
noticeable
occasionally
occurrence
pastime
perseverance
personnel
playwright
possession
precede
principal
principle
privilege
pronunciation
publicly
questionnaire
receive
receipt
recommend
reference
referred
relevant
restaurant
rhyme
rhythm
schedule
separate
sergeant

GEEK GLOSSARY

Heteronyms are words that are spelled the same, but differ in meaning and pronunciation. Examples are alternate (ALT-er-nit) or (ALT-er-NAIT).

GEEKOID

Ben Franklin took great interest in the promotion of spelling reform and proposed a phonetic system for spelling English. His new alphabet consisted of all the lowercase letters of the Latin alphabet, minus c, j, w, x, and y, which he thought were redundant, plus six new letters for sounds. The other letters all adhered to the principle of one symbol per one sound. He commissioned a type foundry to prepare a suitable type including the six new letters, but soon abandoned the project. The only other person to show an interest in the work was Noah Webster of dictionary fame.

superintendent
supersede
threshold
twelfth
tyranny
until
vaccine
vacuum
villain
weather
weird

- Good writing requires properly spelled words.

- Poor spelling can make even good writing look questionable.

- Do not rely exclusively on your spell check to catch misspelled words. It will not alert you to legitimate words used out of context.

THE NITTY-GRITTY ON NUMBERS

Writers are often confused about whether to express numbers with numerals or whether to spell them out in words. Here are some guidelines to help answers questions about this.

There are two general thoughts on guidelines for expressing numbers. Both are simple.

Some experts say to express numbers one through one hundred in words.

- Tim's poll showed <u>eighty-three</u> people in favor of the change.
- All but <u>fifteen</u> of the girls were able to stay for the movie.

Cardinal numbers are actual whole numbers (1, 2, 3, etc.). **Ordinal numbers** indicate position in a series (first, second, third, etc.).

The main concern should be to express numbers with consistency. Treat them the same each time.

Use the same guidelines for expressing ordinal numbers.

- It was the <u>forty-third</u> meeting of the two teams.
- Ms. Green's <u>ninetieth</u> birthday was reported in the newspaper.

Other authorities recommend that you spell out only numbers one through ten. Whichever works best for you, just be consistent.

- Half of the **16** team members were absent.

Spell out numbers that begin a sentence.

- **Twenty-three** men joined in to repair the damaged roof.
- **Two thousand, one hundred fifteen** children attended the school. (Awkward)
- Last year, **2,115** children attended the school. (Better)

GEEKOID

When spelling out numbers that begin a sentence if the number is long, or spelling it out would be awkward, reword the sentence so that the numbers come elsewhere in the sentence.

Round numbers and approximations should be spelled out.

- Over **four thousand people** attended the concert.

When two numbers appear side by side, spell one of them out for clarity.

- There were 2 3-bedroom apartments advertised in the newspaper. (Awkward)
- There were **two 3-bedroom** apartments advertised in the newspaper. (Better)

For expressing physical quantities in nontechnical material, continue to spell out numbers and quantities according to the rules above—choose whether you will spell out one through ten, or one through one hundred, and be consistent.

- The new car quickly sped to <u>80</u> miles per hour.
- The new car quickly sped to <u>eighty</u> miles per hour.

Use your own common sense to decide when physical quantities might be best expressed in numerals.

GEEKOID

Round numbers and approximations greater than one million may be expressed with a combination of numbers and words.

- Over 3 million people were affected by the new regulations.

- The thermometer on Christmas Day read <u>23</u> degrees.

Percentages are always expressed in numerals.

- The numbers of students out sick rose to <u>35</u> percent.

For times of day, write out times when they are given in even hours, half, and quarter hours.

- Our airplane is scheduled to leave at <u>three</u> <u>thirty</u> tomorrow.
- Can you be here at <u>eight</u> <u>o'clock</u> in the morning?

Specific times are written in numerals.

GEEKOID

When you use the word **o'clock**, spell out the numeral.

- The train did not leave until <u>6:25</u> Tuesday night.

- There are times when numbers should be written out as words, and times when they should be expressed as numerals.

- In general, numbers one through ninety-nine should be spelled out, though some authorities suggest spelling out only one through nine.

- Whichever plan is chosen, consistency is the main factor. Do the same thing each time no matter what you choose to do.

- When two numbers appear together (two 2-bedroom units), spell out one of the numbers for clarity.

- Specific times of day are expressed in numerals. Hours, half hours, and quarter hours are expressed in words.

WRITE THIS WAY

Just needing to write doesn't mean you can easily sit down and do it. If you're looking for a blueprint for writing, here are some suggestions that may be helpful.

Getting Started

It may help to have a plan as you begin to write. Here are some tried-and-true steps to help you get from one point to the next.

- Know why you are writing. Defining your purpose will help you identify ideas you want to include.
- Identify your audience. Knowing who will be reading what you write will help you know what should be included, and how your reader will best understand it.
- Get ideas out on paper. You may try making an outline or developing a list of questions that your work should answer.

GEEK Speak:

"If a person wishes to write in a clear style, let him first be clear in his thoughts."

Goethe

GEEKOID

Many people find the stream of consciousness method effective for generating ideas. This is also called free writing. Think about what you want to express and type out related ideas as you think, without stopping. Do not edit as you go. The most important thing is to get out as many ideas as possible.

- Group related ideas together. These groups will form your paragraphs.
- Put your ideas in a logical sequence. Now your document is beginning to take shape.
- Fill in the ideas with some details, and begin to form paragraphs.
- Write an introduction and a conclusion based on the ideas you've just developed.
- Read through your work and edit, edit, edit. Write transitions to join your paragraphs and smooth the way between ideas.
- Make it perfect. Check for typos and errors.

GUERRILLA GEEK

The **pilcrow** (¶), commonly referred to as the paragraph symbol, is a non-alphabetic symbol used to indicate where you should indent or indent and begin a new paragraph.

GUERRILLA GEEK

Even though an introductory paragraph will begin your work, many writers find it easier to write this important beginning after all other parts have been done. This way, you can see what it is you're introducing.

Style

Now that you have your ideas on paper, go back over it and polish it to perfection.

- Use plain English. Do not try to impress your reader(s) with big words. Just say what you have to say.

A good guideline for choosing words in your writing is to not write words on paper that you wouldn't say in conversation. That means, don't say, "Pursuant to," when what you mean is "After."

- Try for a conversational tone. Of course there are times for more formal writing, but usually, you should write like you were talking to the person directly.
- Use a variety of words, especially verbs. Be particularly careful of using the same unusual words repeatedly. They will stand out like sore thumbs. (Try to avoid clichés, too!)

GEEK GLOSSARY

Here's a symbol that may be handy as you edit: it's called a **caret** (^). It's an inverted v-shaped mark used to show that something should be inserted where indicated.

GEEKOID

Clichés are phrases that have been so commonly used that they have been overused. Employing clichés in your writing shows a lack of imagination and originality.

- Use active voice whenever possible. Use passive voice on a limited basis.
- Make sure you use the correct words to express yourself. Don't use **their** when you mean **there.**
- If you are unsure about your grammar, look up the correct way to express yourself, or reword. Rewording is always a great option.
- After you've worked on writing a document for a while, you may lose objectivity about it. Lay the work aside for a while, then come back to it and read it with fresh eyes to catch errors or unclear passages.

GEEK*Speak:*

"No passion in the world is equal to the passion to alter someone else's draft."
H.G. Wells

- Have someone else read through your work for an objective read.
- Have a good dictionary on hand and use it often. Not only will it help you with basic spelling, but it will often offer tips on usage.
- Check your work carefully for misspelled words, correct punctuation, and format particulars.

GEEK AT A GLANCE

- Good writing requires effort and patience. There are logical steps to follow as you begin to work on your writing skills.

- Once you have created your first draft, there are particular things you can to do make your work clear and easy to read.

INDEX